INTRODUC

MW01698032

Welcome to the beginner Piano Lesson Book. The Book contains 50 fun and easy popular piano songs to play. It also teaches the basics of reading sheet music (measure, bar lines, time signatures, duration of notes, tie, repeats etc.) and lays the foundation to sight reading of sheet music. The book starts with easy to play songs and then gradually increases the difficulties. Therefore, it is highly recommended to start with the simple melodies.
The Book is designed by an experienced musician to accelerate and simplify your piano learning skill. Most of the songs include piano note chart diagram with corresponding keys. This will help to identify and memorize notes easily. Each of the notes in the book are color coded to recognize the notes without effort. We recommend practicing every day for 10-15 min to build confidence and hand co-ordination. It is also recommended to use the color-coded piano stickers with the book. Students can use these color-coded notes to quickly recognize the notes and to easily memorize them.

Good Luck with Piano Learning!!!

QMG

Quality Music Gear

DVN Products LLC
9262 Raveena Road, Unit A6
Twinsburg OH 44087
Email: dvnproduct@gmail.com
Tel: 440-701-6426

ISBN-13: 978-1639011384
Designed and printed in the USA

Table of Contents

Music Theory	3
Ring Around the Rosie	4
Rain Rain Go Away/The Hunting we will go	5
This Old Man	6
The Halloween song	7
Are You Sleeping	8
The Wheels on the Bus	9
Happy Birthday	10
Jingle Bells	11
Mary Had a Little Lamb	12
Twinkle Twinkle	13
Alphabet Song	14
London Bridge	15
Baa Baa Black Sheep	16
Old MacDonald Had a Farm	18
Ode to Joy	20
Amazing Grace	22
Hot Cross Buns	23
Alouette (French Folk Song)	24
Yankee Doodle	26
Lullaby	28
Hush Little Baby	30
Skip to My Lou	31
Kum Ba Yah	32
The Muffin Man	33
We Wish You a Merry Christmas	34
Girls and Boys	36
A Tisket A Tasket	37
Bingo	38
Scarborough Fair	39
Oranges and Lemons	40
Pop Goes the Weasel	41
Coming Round the Mountain	42
Silent Night	44
English Country Garden	46
Humpty Dumpty	48
Row Row Row your Boat	49
If You're Happy	50
The Itsy Bitsy Spider	51
The Farmer in the Dell	52
Head Shoulders Knees and Toes	53
I Come from Alabama	54
Lavender's Blue	55
Polly Put the Kettle On	56
Molly Malone	57
Tom Dooly	58
Red River Valley	59
FÜr Elise	60
Camptown Races	62
Hickory Dickory Dock	63
When the Saints Go Marching In	64

MUSIC THEORY

Time Signature

2 ← 2 beats to each measure
4 ← A Quarter note gets one beat

3 ← 3 beats to each measure
4 ← A Quarter note gets one beat

4 ← 4 beats to each measure
4 ← A Quarter note gets one beat

6 ← 6 beats to each measure
8 ← A eight note gets one beat

Measure and Barline:

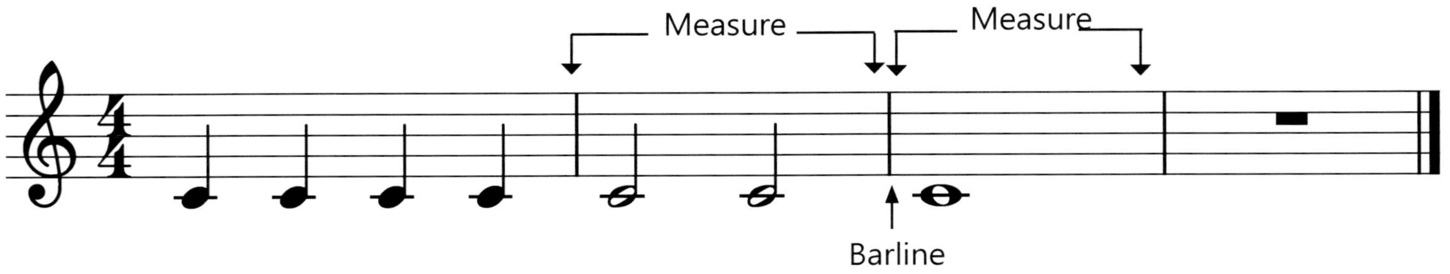
Measure
Measure
Barline

Note Values

Whole Note	Dotted Half Note	Half Note	Quarter Note	Eighth Note
Count "1-2-3-4"	Count "1-2-3"	Count "1-2"	Count "1"	Count "1/2"

Rest Values

Rest values refer to the duration of silence in music. When you see these rest value simply do not play the notes but count for correspoinding beats.

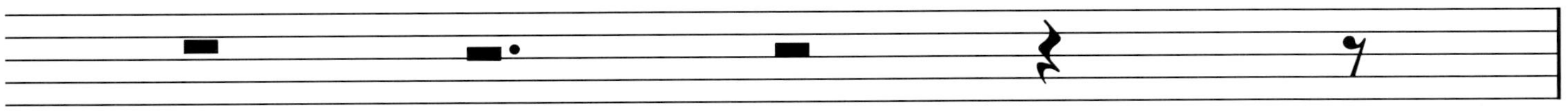

Whole Rest	Dotted Half Rest	Half Rest	Quarter Rest	Eighth Rest
Count "1-2-3-4"	Count "1-2-3"	Count "1-2"	Count "1"	Count "1/2"
silence for four beats	silence for three beats	silence for two beats	silence for one beat	silence for half beat

Ring Around the Rosie

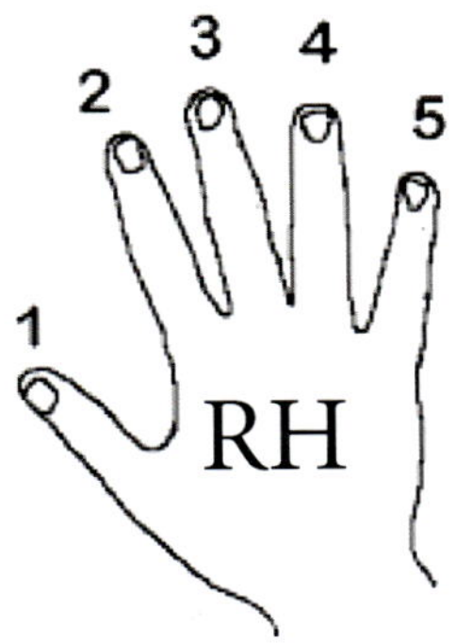
1
2
3
4
5
RH

RH - Right Hand
fingering numbers

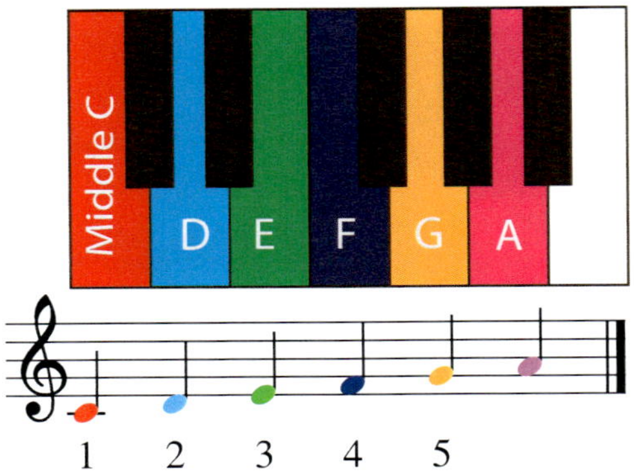
Middle C
D
E
F
G
A
1
2
3
4
5

Finger numbers show on top of the measure and use the correct fingering.

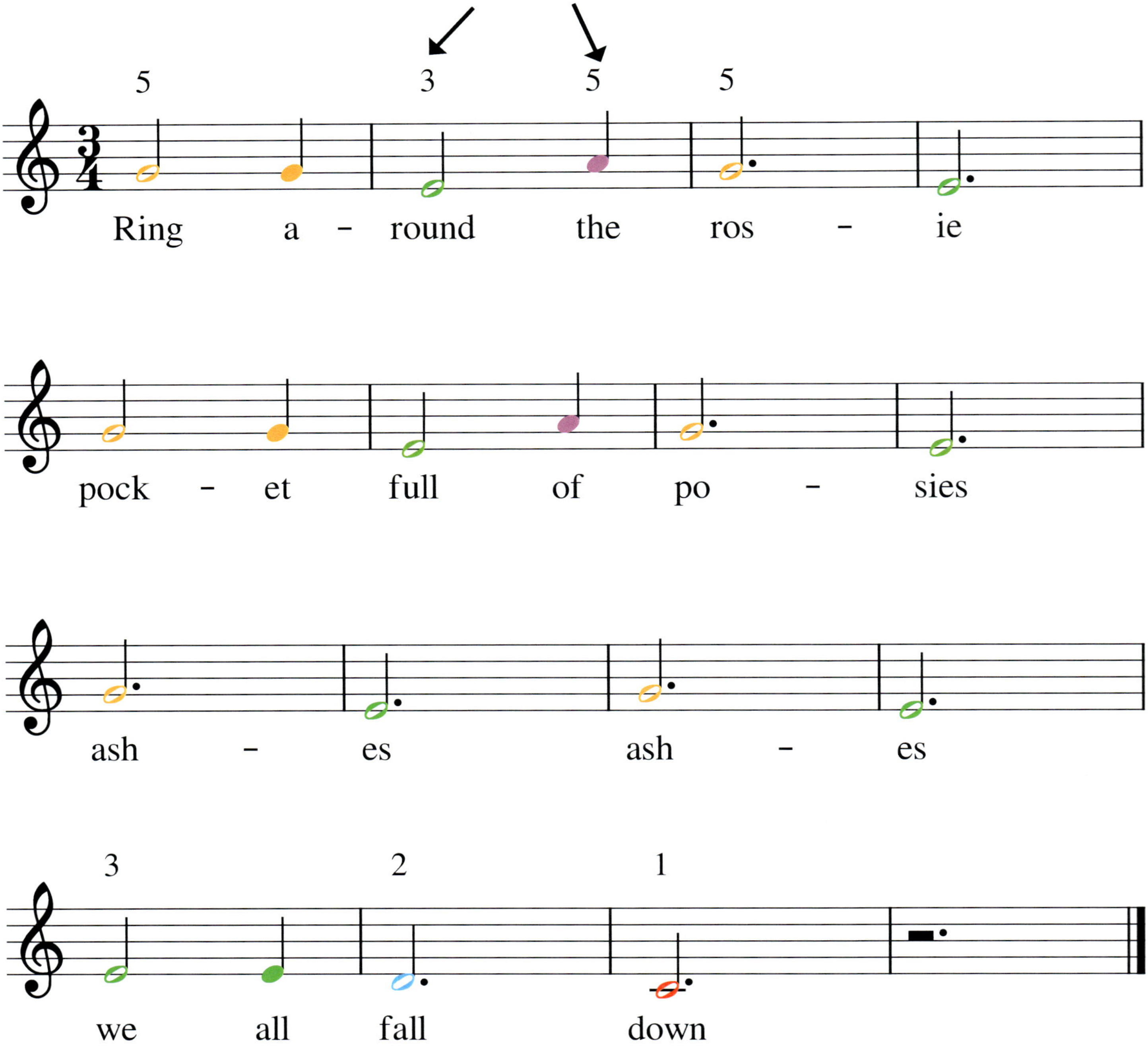
5 3 5 5
Ring a - round the ros - ie
pock - et full of po - sies
ash - es ash - es
3 2 1
we all fall down

Rain Rain Go Away

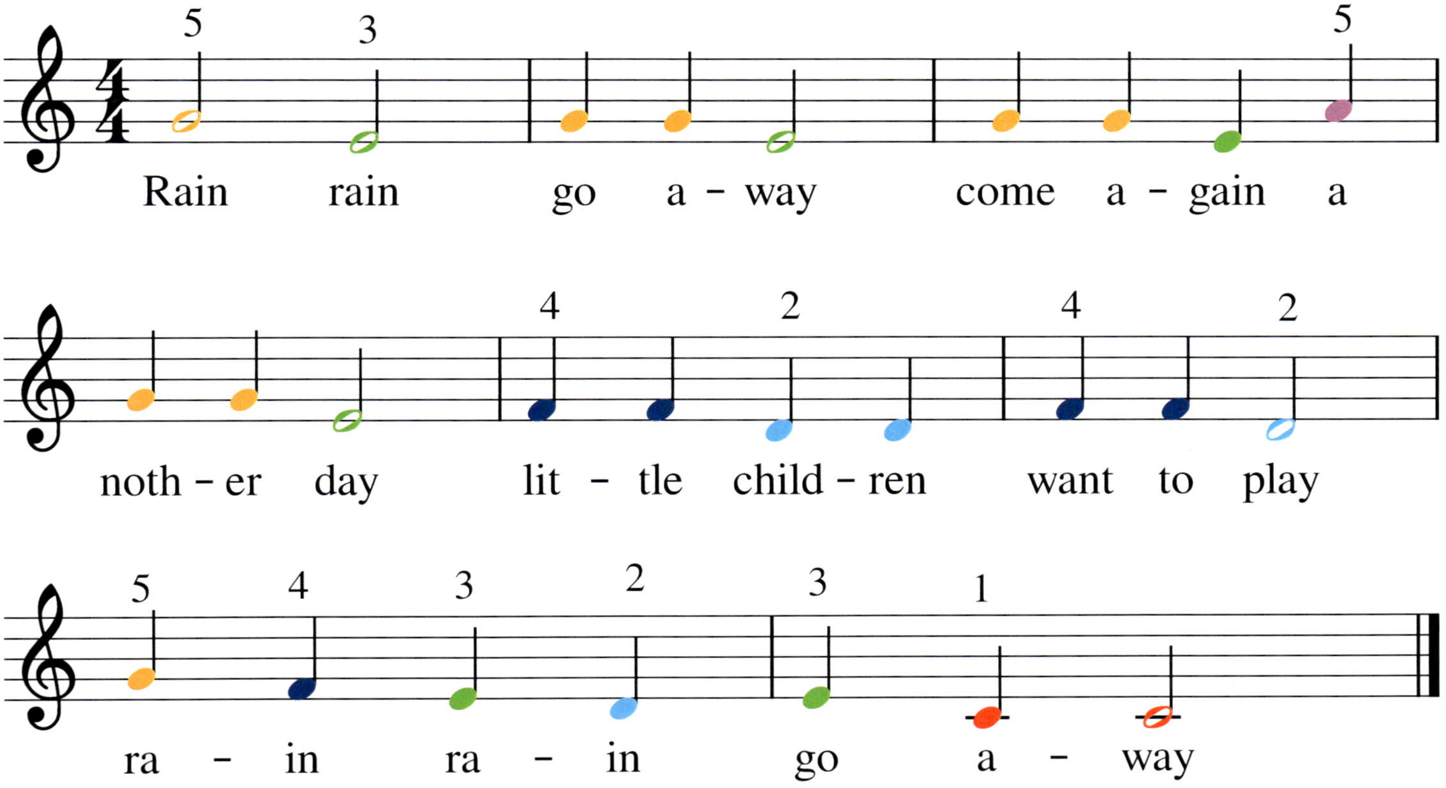
Rain rain go a – way come a – gain a
noth – er day lit – tle child – ren want to play
ra – in ra – in go a – way

A Hunting We Will Go

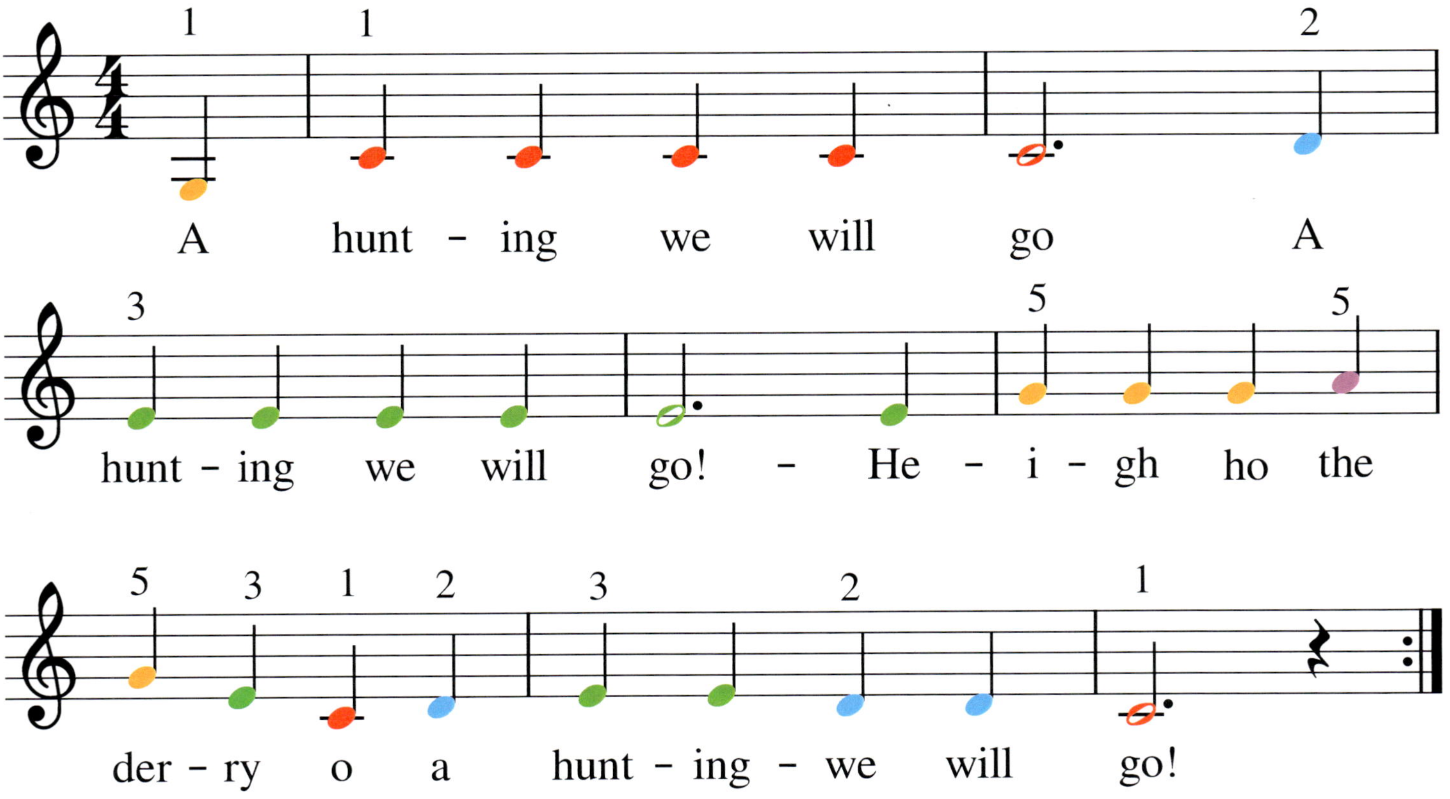
A hunt – ing we will go A
hunt – ing we will go! – He – i – gh ho the
der – ry o a hunt – ing – we will go!

This Old Man

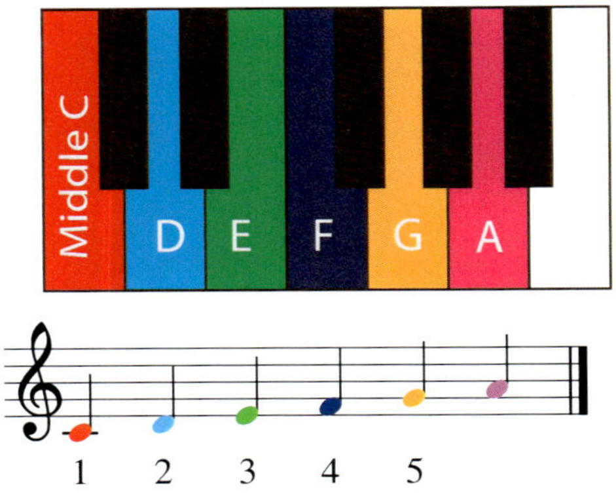
Middle C
D
E
F
G
A
1 2 3 4 5

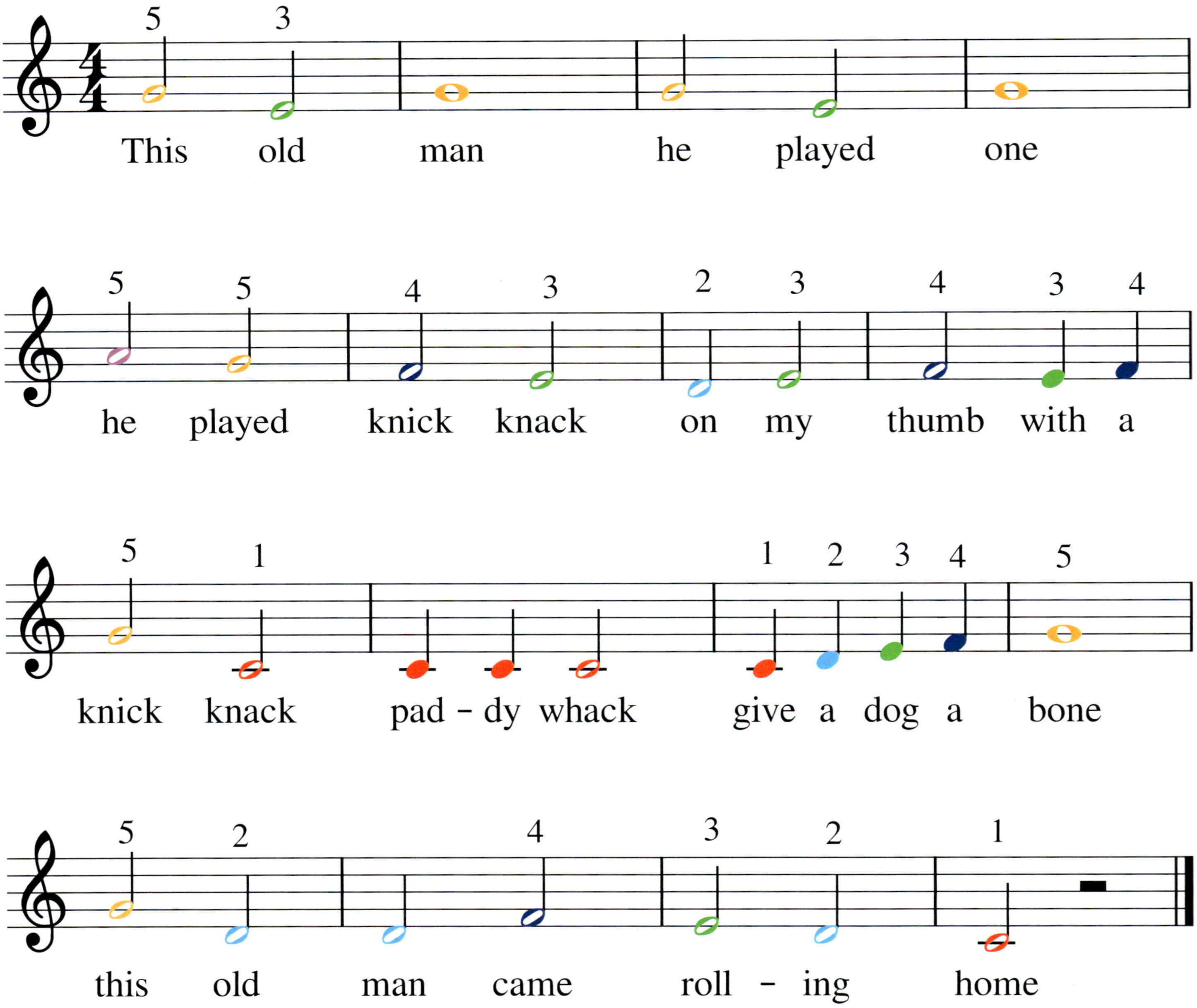
5 3
This old man he played one
5 5 4 3 2 3 4 3 4
he played knick knack on my thumb with a
5 1 1 2 3 4 5
knick knack pad - dy whack give a dog a bone
5 2 4 3 2 1
this old man came roll - ing home

The Halloween Song

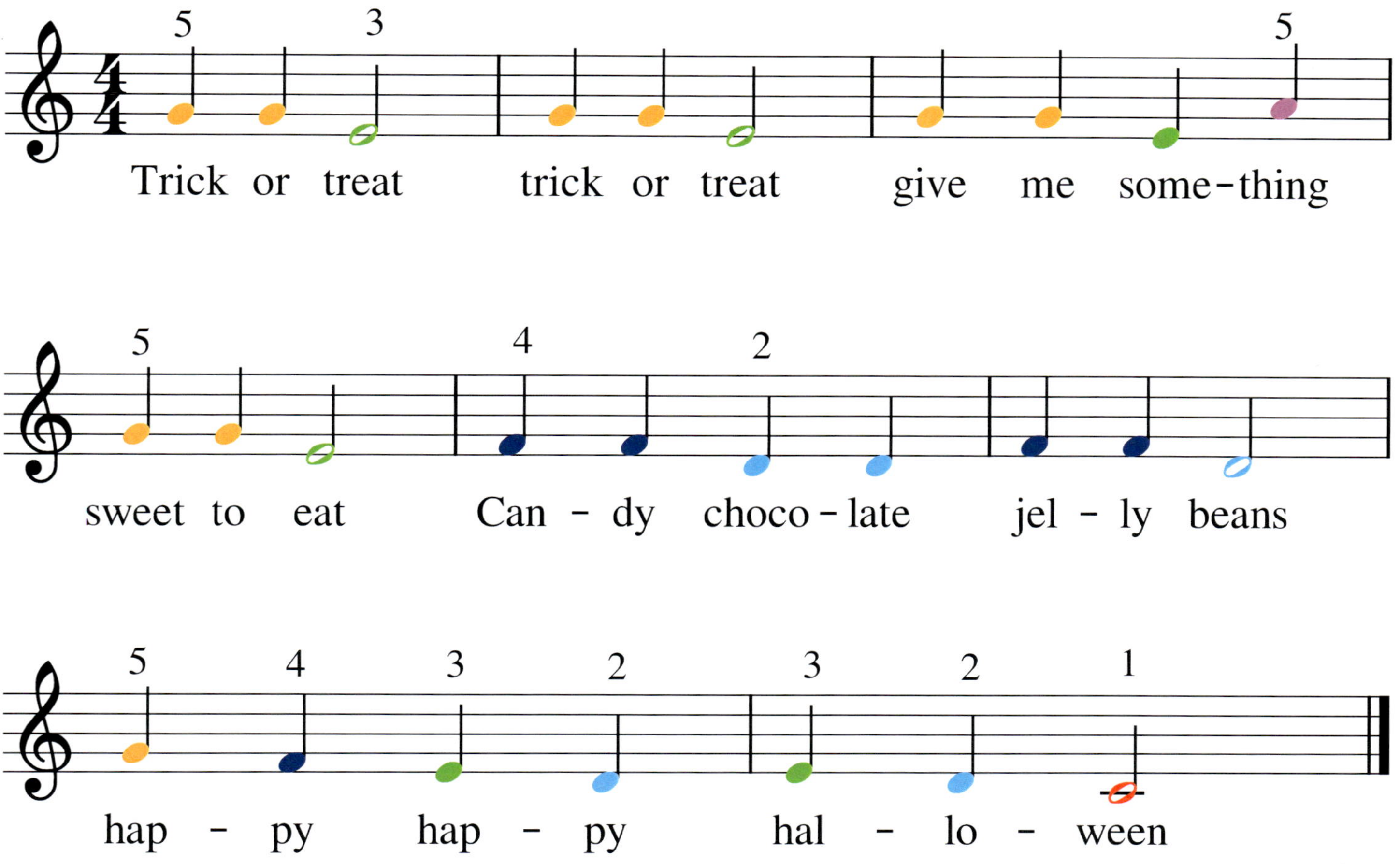
5 3 5
Trick or treat trick or treat give me some-thing
5 4 2
sweet to eat Can - dy choco - late jel - ly beans
5 4 3 2 3 2 1
hap - py hap - py hal - lo - ween

The Grand Staff

Treble Staff and Bass Staff joined together, with a Brace is called Grand Staff. In Grand Staff, treble staff notes play using your right hand (RH) and bass staff notes play using your left hand (LH).

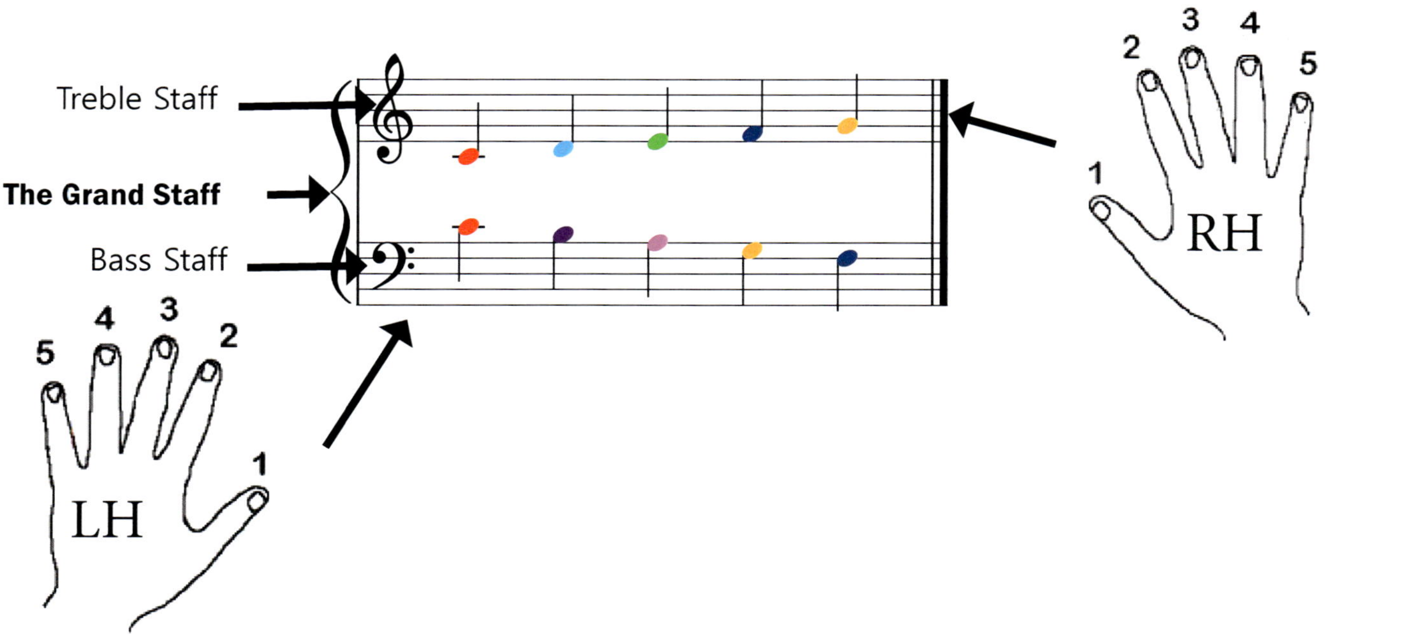
Treble Staff
The Grand Staff
Bass Staff
1 2 3 4 5
RH
5 4 3 2 1
LH

Are You Sleeping

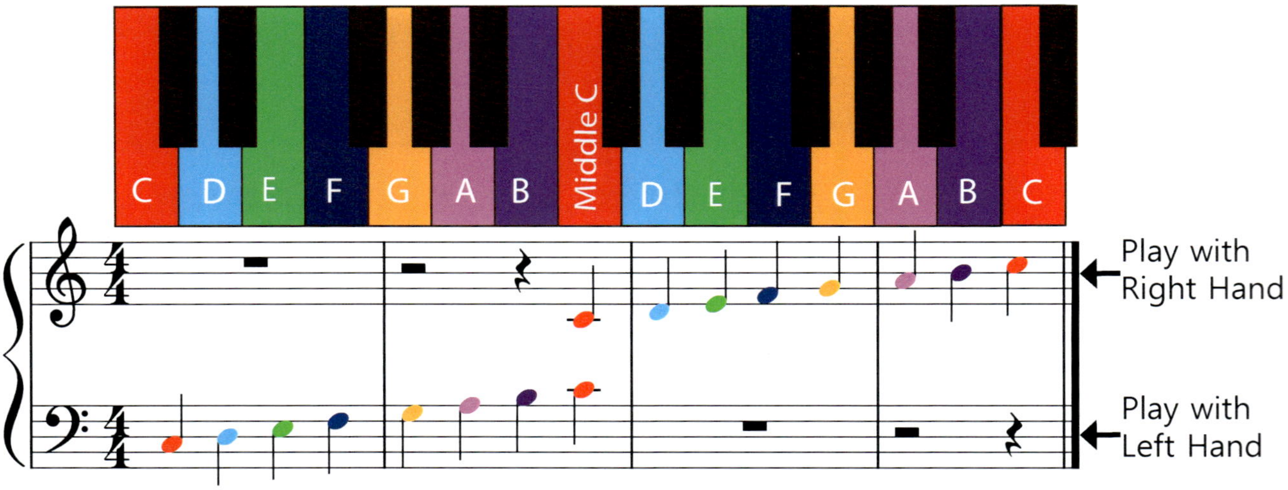
C D E F G A B Middle C D E F G A B C
Play with Right Hand
Play with Left Hand

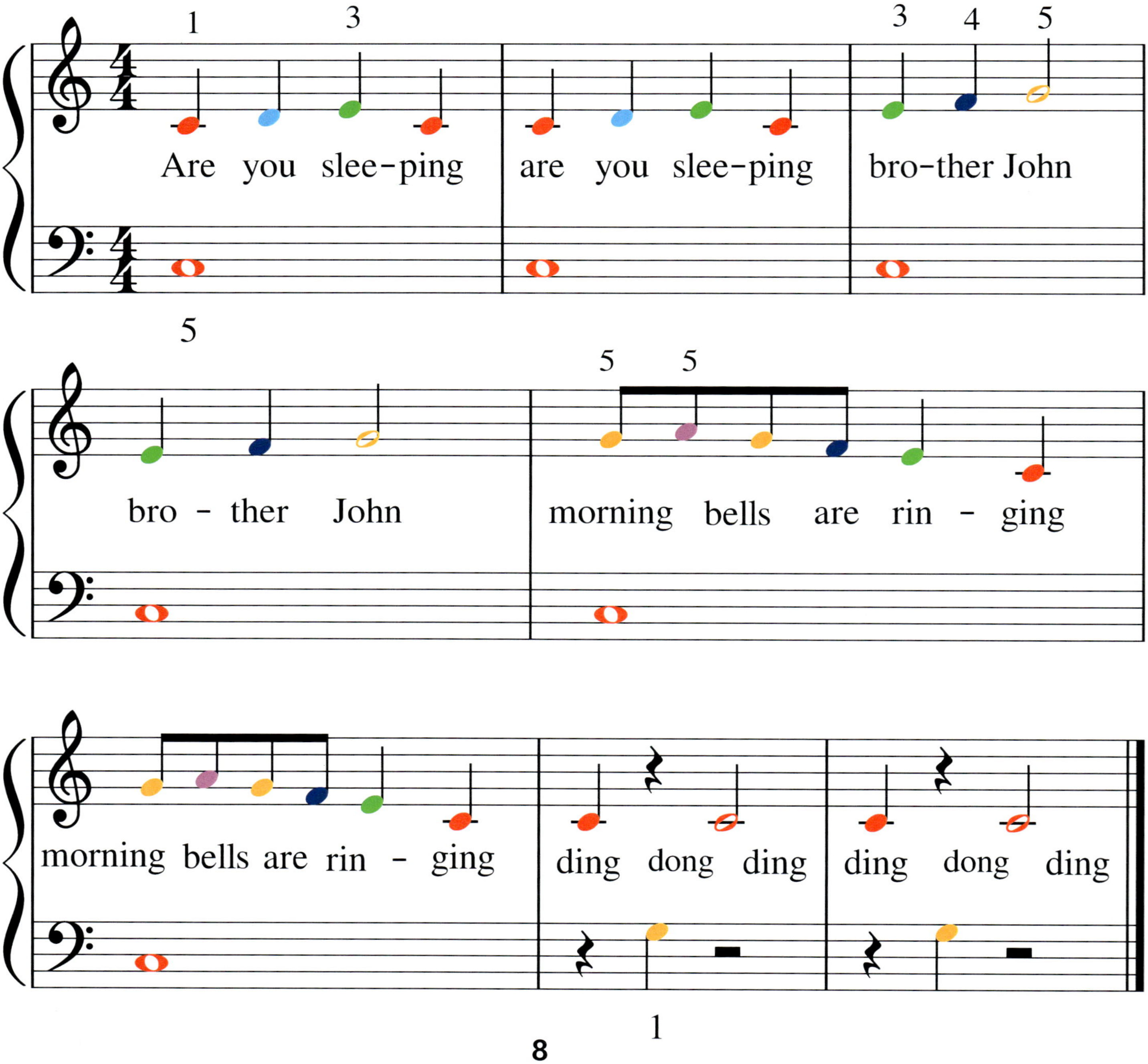
Are you slee-ping are you slee-ping bro-ther John
bro - ther John
morning bells are rin - ging
morning bells are rin - ging
ding dong ding
ding dong ding

The Wheels on the Bus

Eighth notes count as 1 & 2 & 3 & 4 &

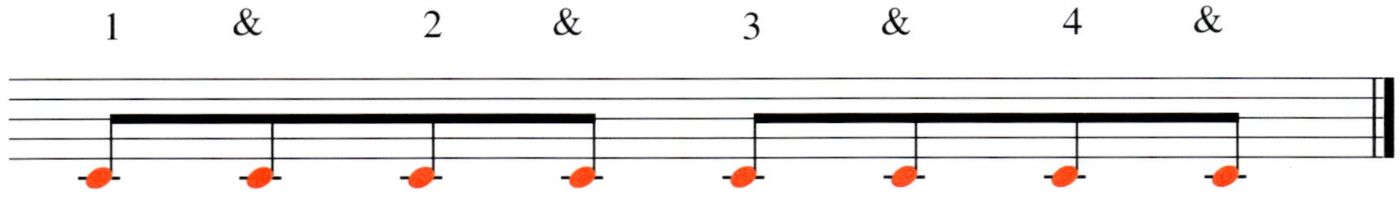
1 & 2 & 3 & 4 &

1 3 5 3 1
The wheels on the bus go round and round
5
2 5 3 1 3
round and round round and round the wheels on the bus go
3 5 5
5 3 1 2 1
round and round all through the town
5

Happy Birthday

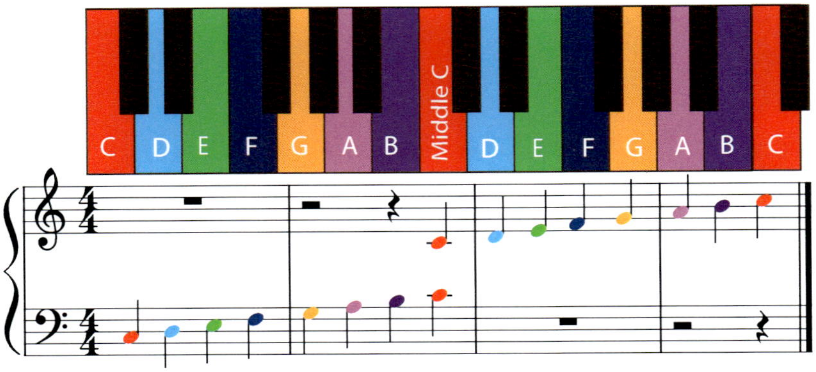
C D E F G A B Middle C D E F G A B C

Hap - py Birth - day to you Hap-py
Birth - day to you Hap-py Birth- day dear
(name) Hap -py Birth - day to you

Jingle Bells

3
3 5 1
1
5
Jin gle bells
Jin gle bells
Jin gle all the
way
4
2 5
1
2
Oh what fun it
is to ride ina
one horse o pen
sleigh oh
Jin gle bells
Jin gle bells
Jin gle all the
way
4
Oh What fun it
is to ride ina
one horse o pen
sleigh

Mary Had a Little Lamb

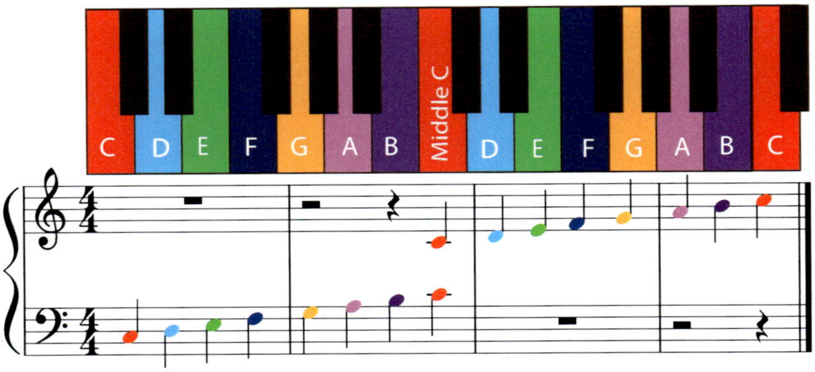
C D E F G A B Middle C D E F G A B C

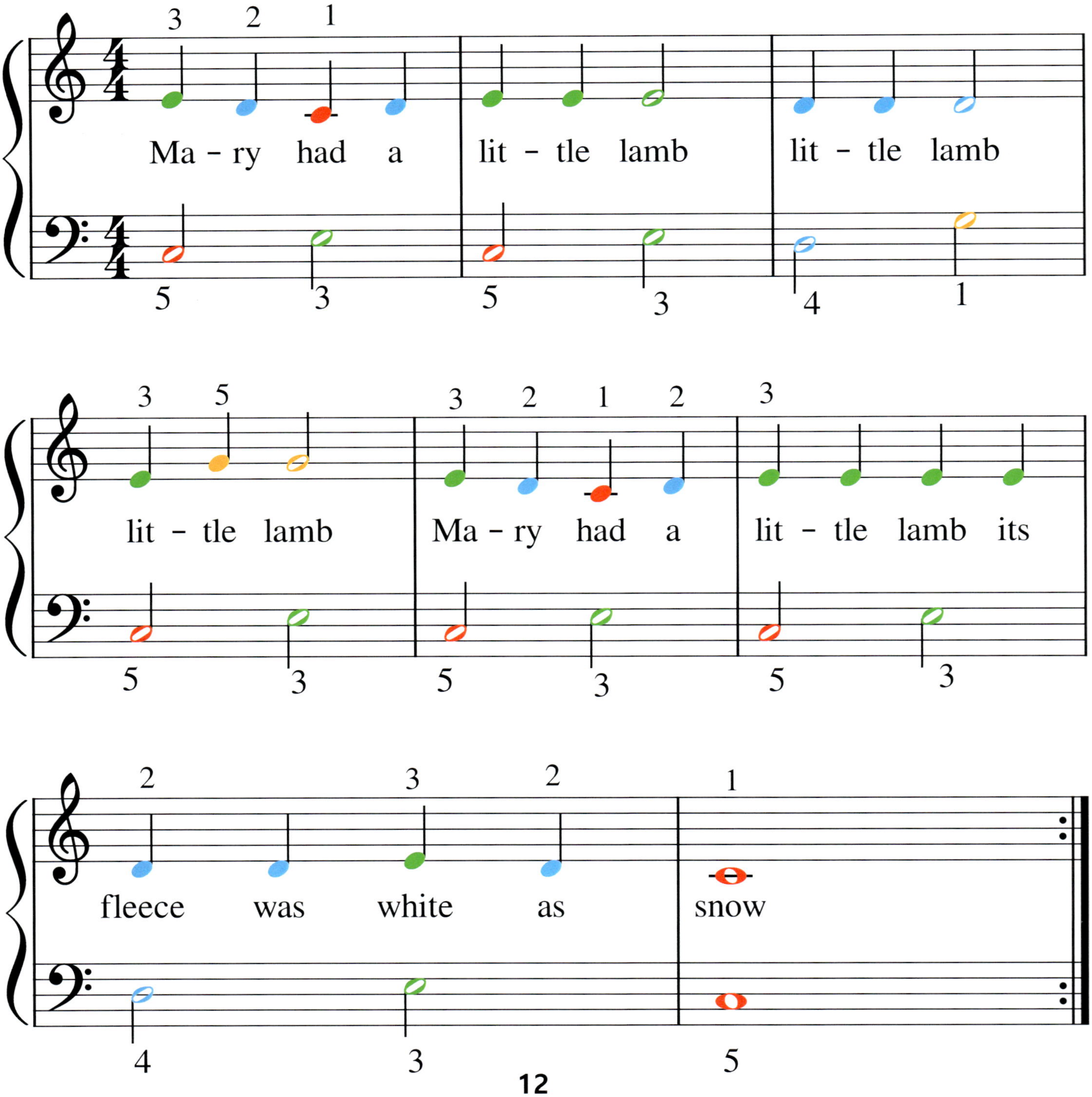
3 2 1
Ma - ry had a lit - tle lamb lit - tle lamb
5 3 5 3 4 1
3 5 3 2 1 2 3
lit - tle lamb Ma - ry had a lit - tle lamb its
5 3 5 3 5 3
2 3 2 1
fleece was white as snow
4 3 5

Twinkle Twinkle

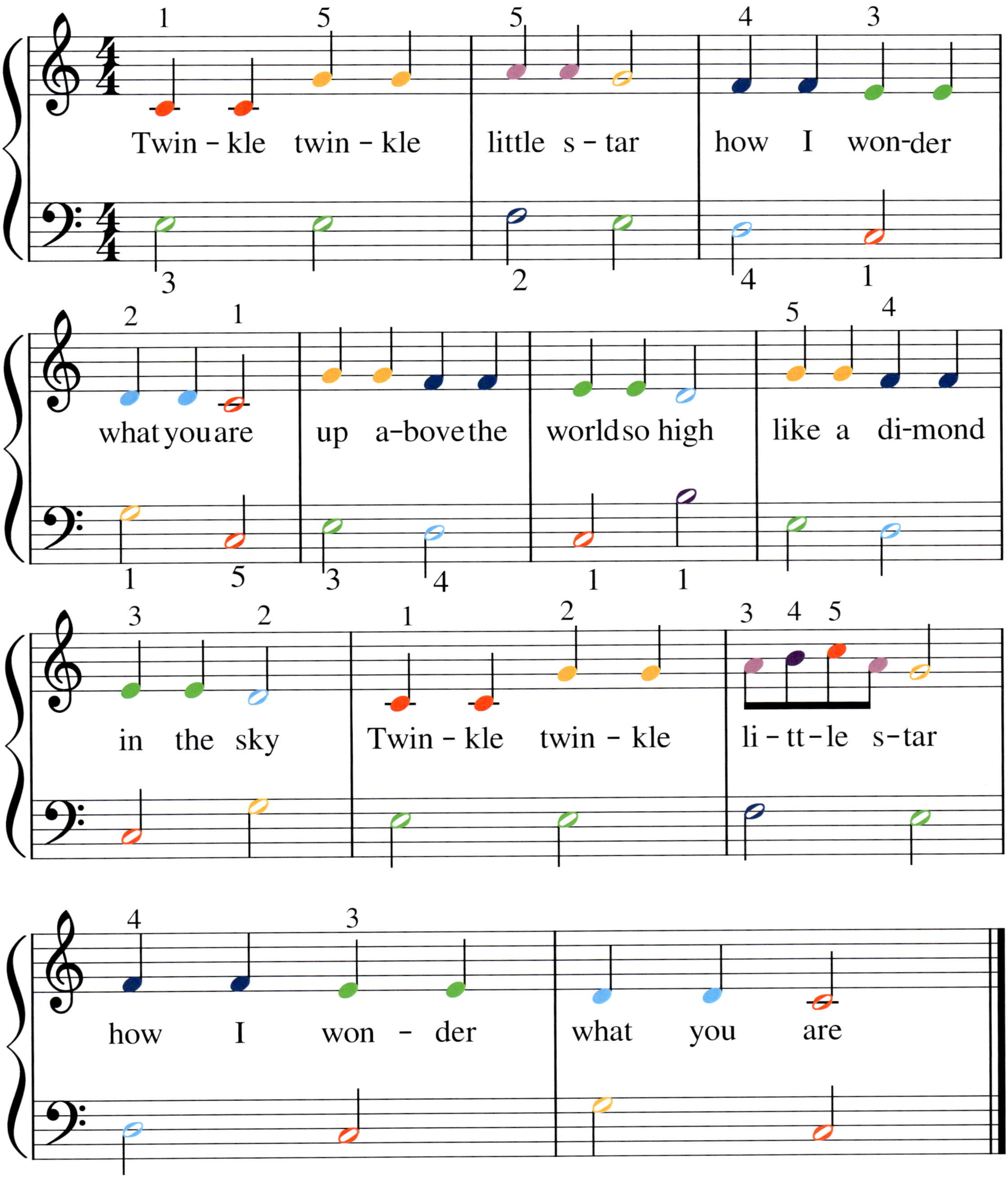
Twin - kle twin - kle little s - tar how I won-der
what you are up a-bove the world so high like a di-mond
in the sky Twin - kle twin - kle li - tt - le s - tar
how I won - der what you are

Alphabet Song

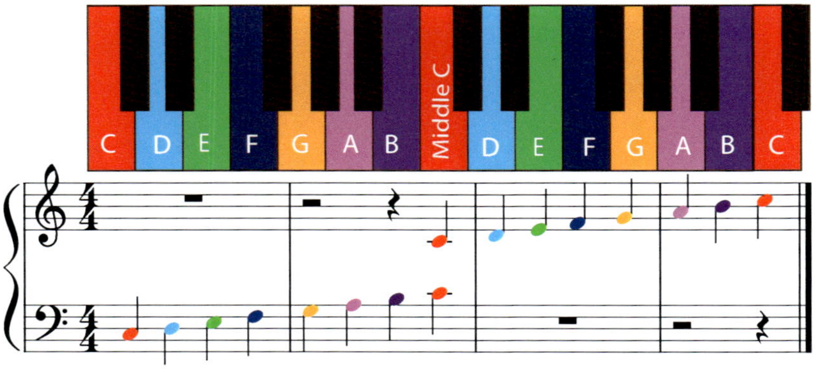
C D E F G A B
Middle C
D E F G A B C

A B C D E F G H I J K L M N O P
Q R S T U V W X Y and Z
Now I know my A B C next time want you sing with me

London Bridge

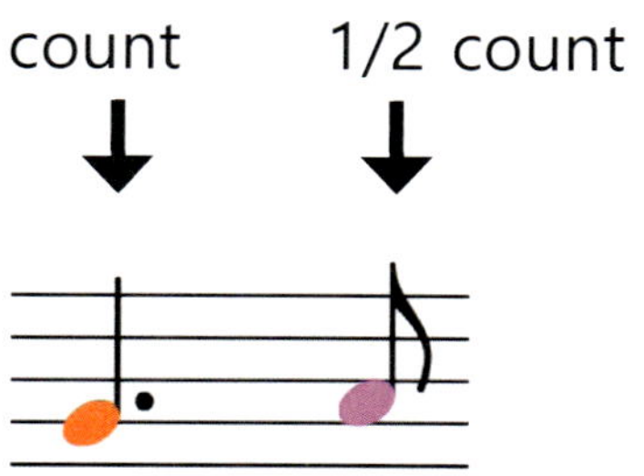
1 1/2 count
1/2 count

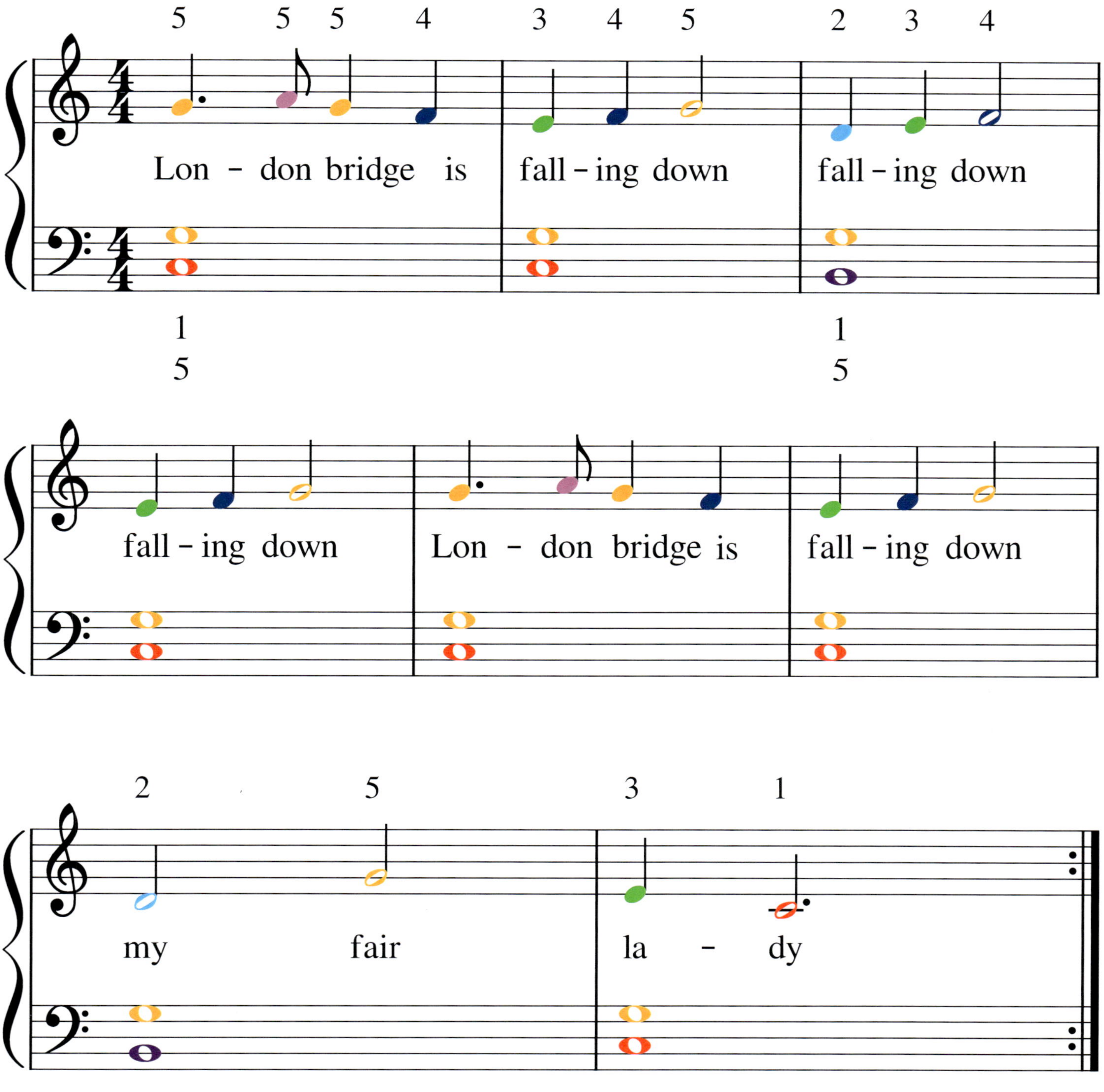
5 5 5 4 3 4 5 2 3 4
Lon - don bridge is fall - ing down fall - ing down
1
5
1
5
fall - ing down Lon - don bridge is fall - ing down
2 5 3 1
my fair la - dy

Baa Baa Black Sheep

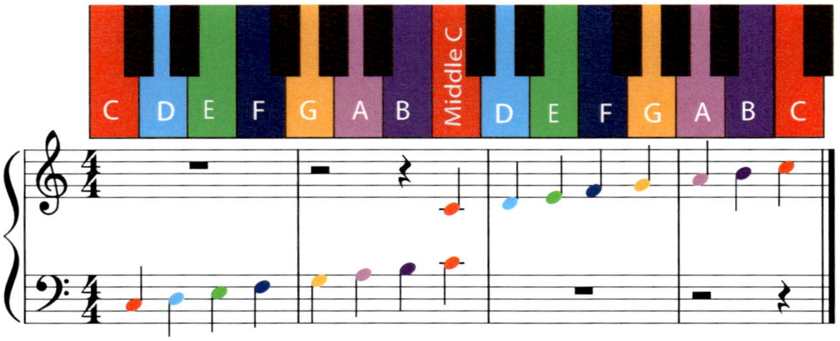
C D E F G A B Middle C D E F G A B C

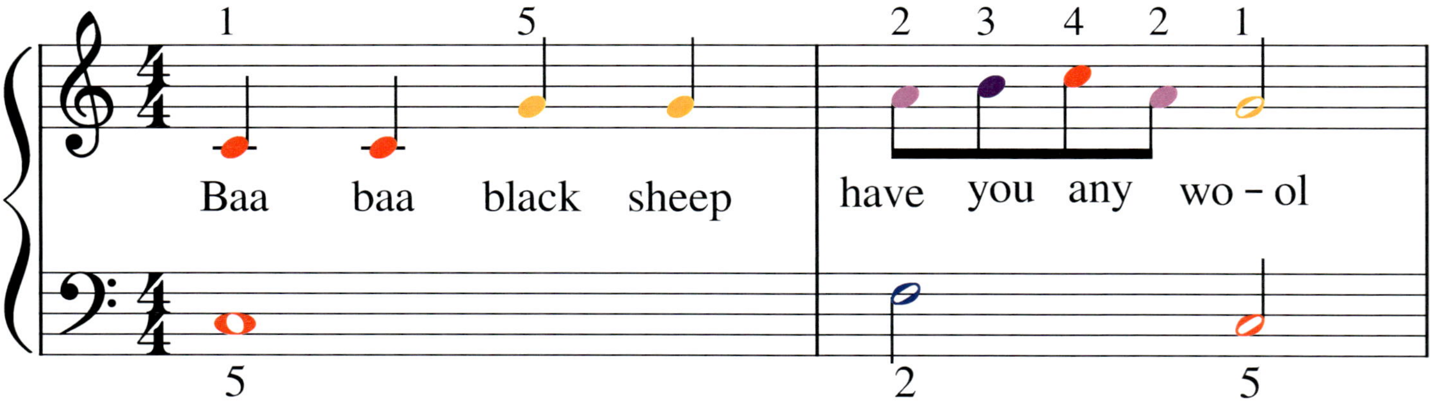
Baa baa black sheep
have you any wo - ol

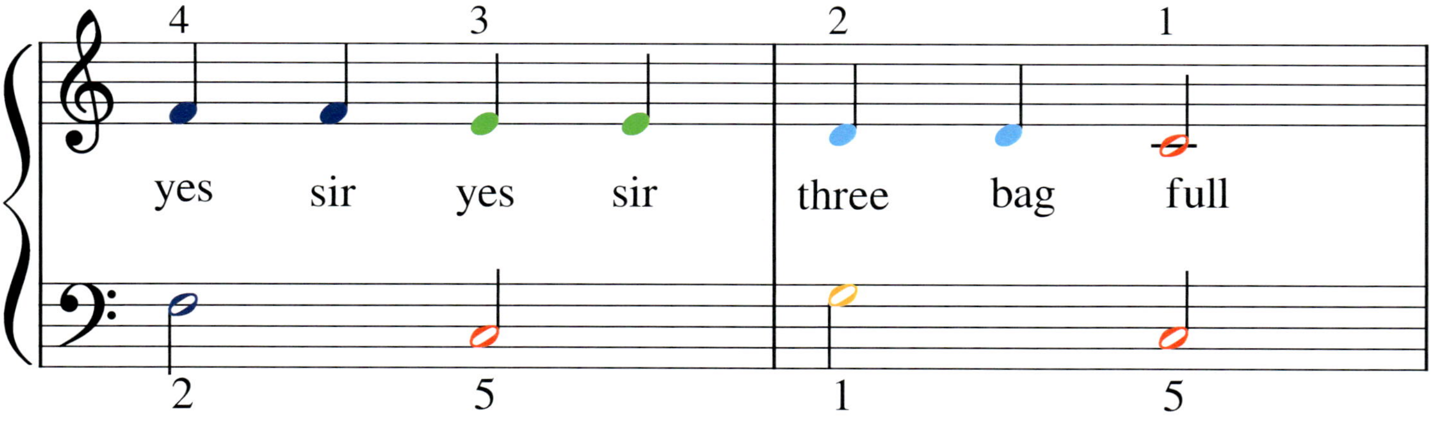
yes sir yes sir
three bag full

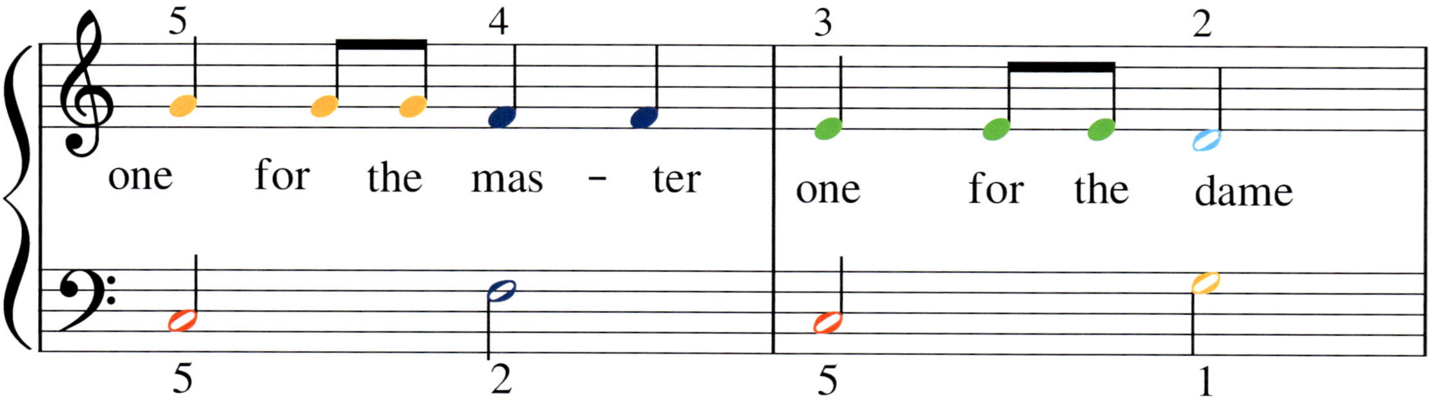
one for the mas - ter
one for the dame

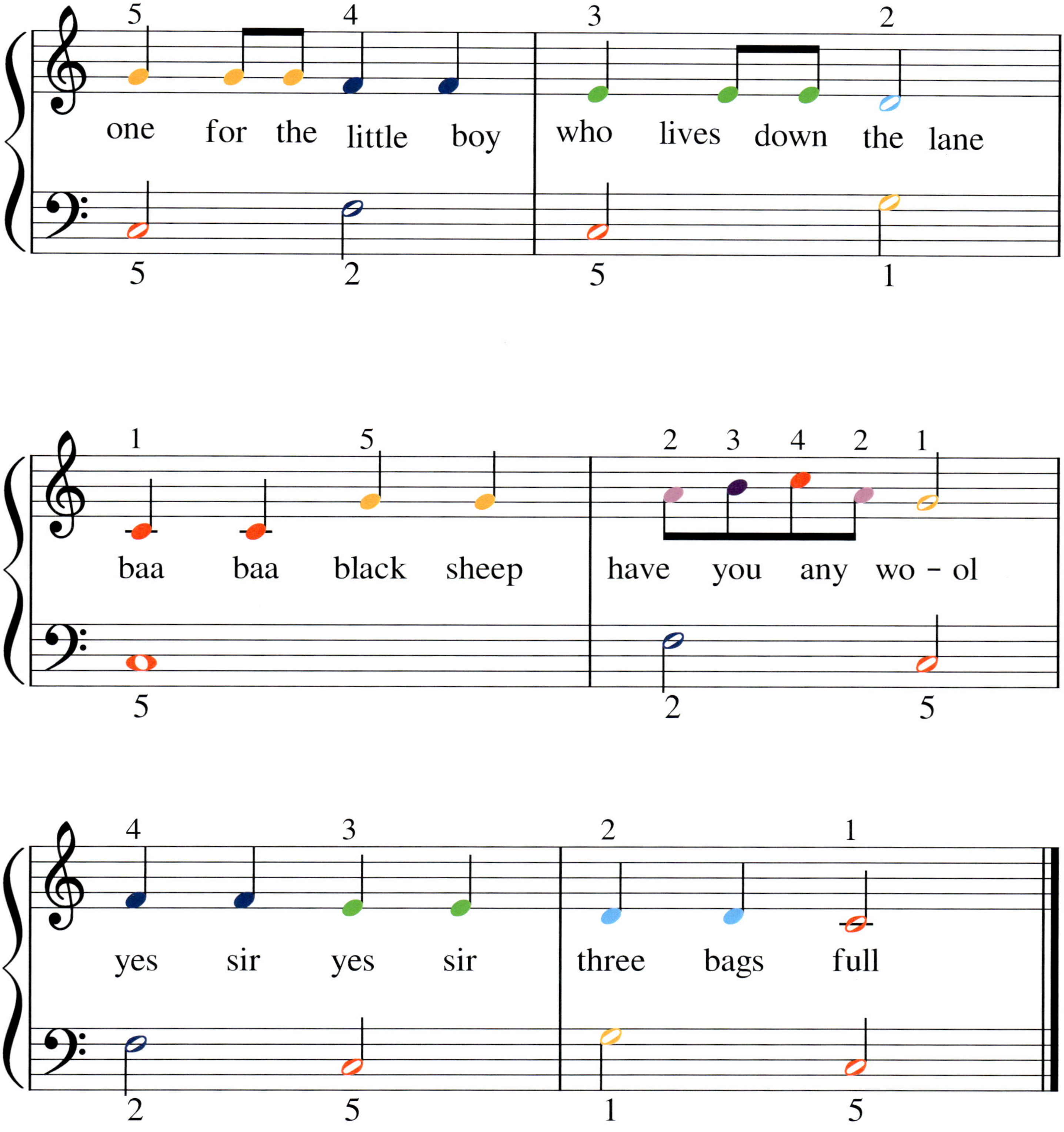
one for the little boy
who lives down the lane
baa baa black sheep
have you any wo – ol
yes sir yes sir
three bags full

Old MacDonald Had a Farm

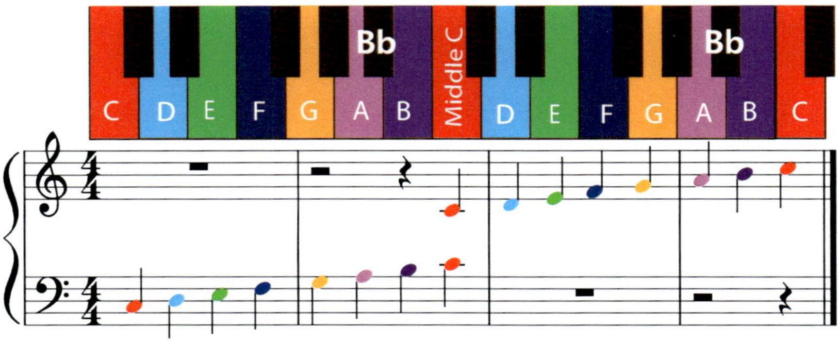
Bb
Bb
C D E F G A B
Middle C
D E F G A B C

Old Mac Don - ald had a farm E - I - E - I
O! And on the farm he had some cows
E - I - E - I O! with a moo - moo here and a

Old MacDonald had a farm song is in 4/4 time signature. Dont forget the **Bb** note.

moo moo there
here a moo there a moo
5 5 5 5
Everywhere moo moo
Old Mac-Don-ald
had a farm
5 5 5 5 5 5 2 5
E - I - E - I
O!
5 1 5

Ode to Joy

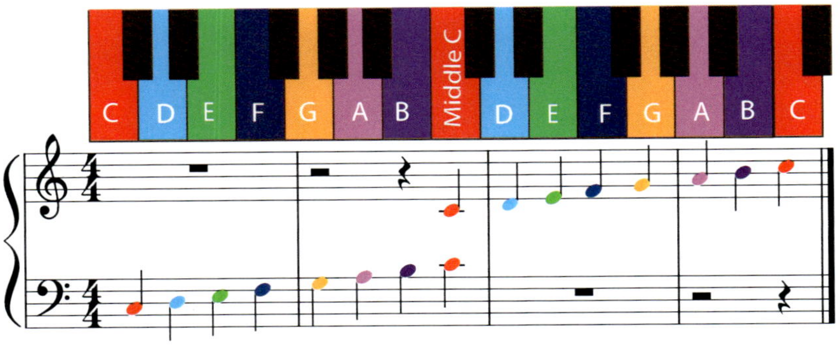
C D E F G A B
Middle C
D E F G A B C

Joy - ful joy - ful
we a dore thee
God of glo - ry

Lord of love
Hearts un fold like
flow'rs be - fore Thee

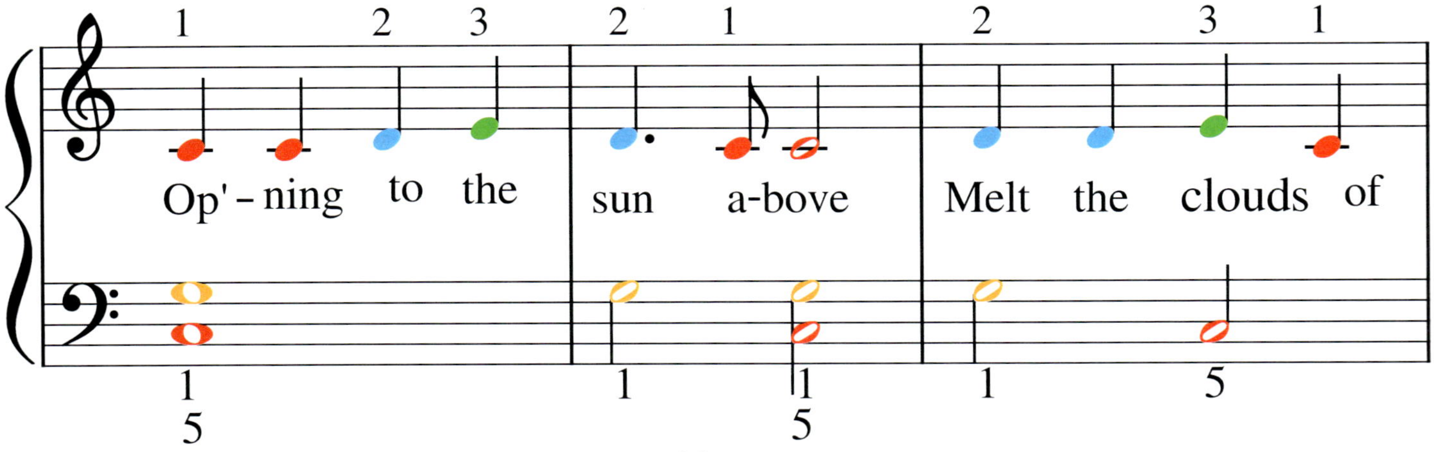
Op' - ning to the
sun a-bove
Melt the clouds of

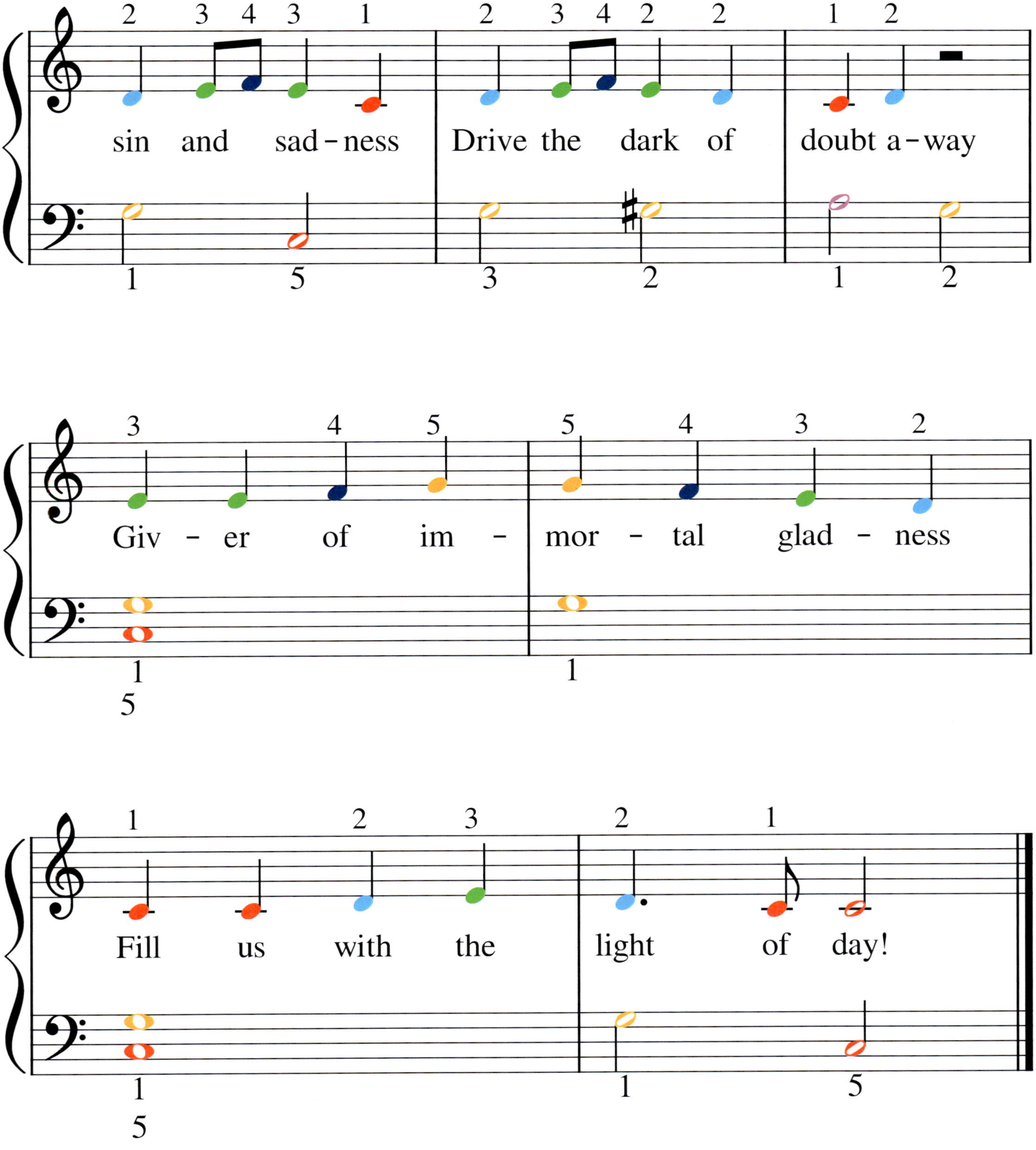
sin and sad-ness
Drive the dark of
doubt a-way
Giv - er of im -
mor - tal glad - ness
Fill us with the
light of day!

Amazing Grace

F#
F#
C D E F G A B
Middle C
D E F G A B C

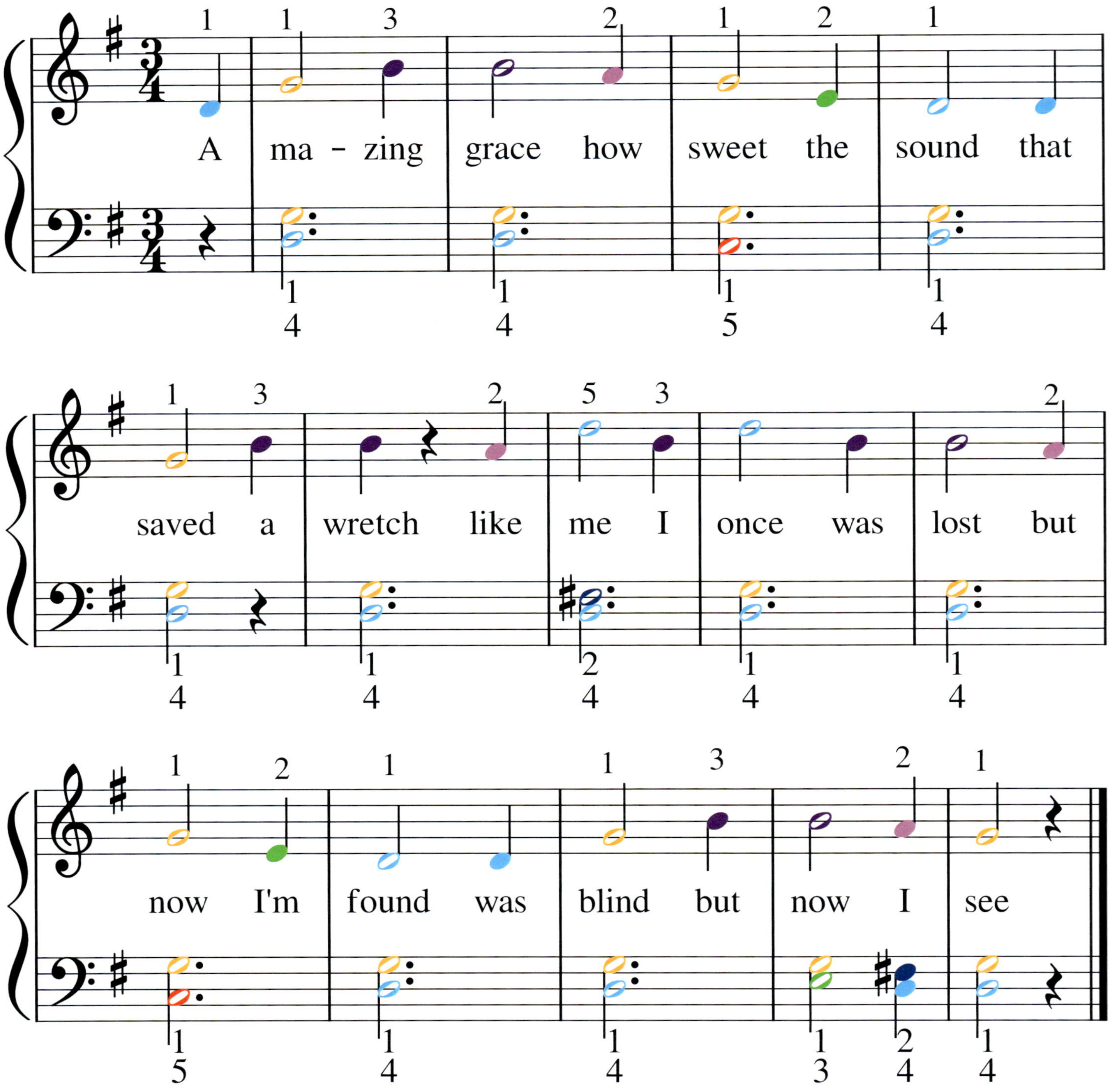
A ma - zing grace how sweet the sound that
saved a wretch like me I once was lost but
now I'm found was blind but now I see

Hot Cross Buns

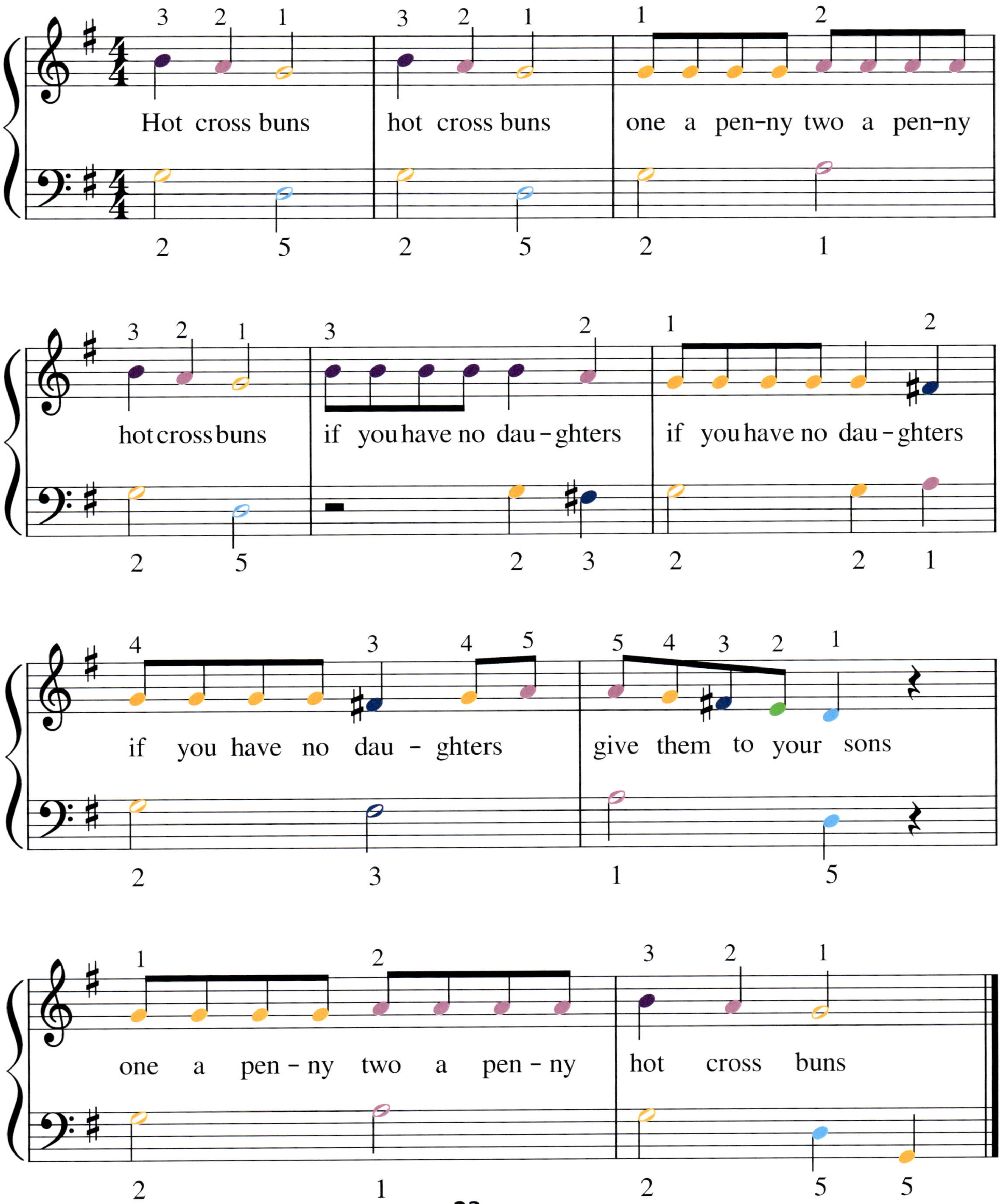
Hot cross buns
hot cross buns
one a pen–ny two a pen–ny
hot cross buns
if you have no dau – ghters
if you have no dau – ghters
if you have no dau – ghters
give them to your sons
one a pen – ny two a pen – ny
hot cross buns

Alouette (French Folk Song)

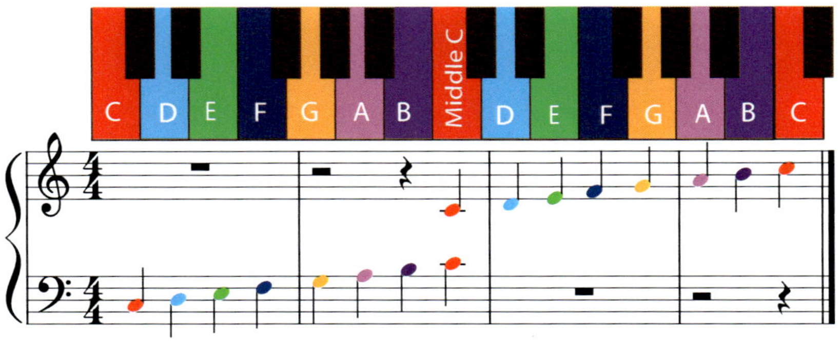
C D E F G A B Middle C D E F G A B C

1 2 3
A lou et te
2 1 2 3 1
gen tille a lou et te
1 5
1 2
1 3
1
1 2 3 3
A lou et te
2 1 2 3 1
je te plu me rai
1 5
1 2
1 3
je te plu me rai la tete
5 4 3 2 1 1 1
Je te plu me rai la tete
5 4 3 2 1 1 1

Et la tete
Et la tete
je te plu me
A lou et te
gentille a lou et
A lou et te
je te plu me rai

Yankee Doodle

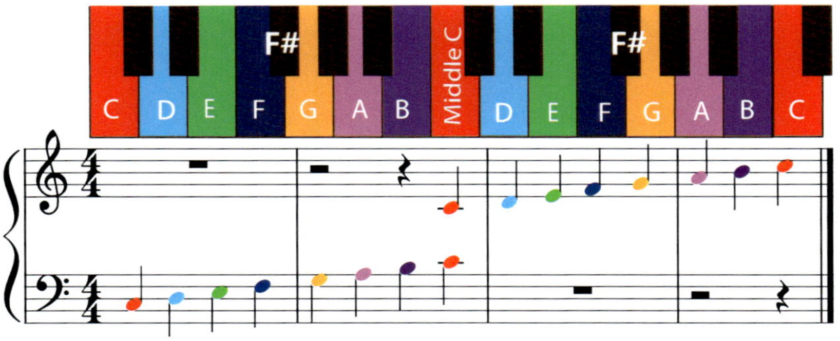
C D E F G A B
F#
Middle C
D E F G A B C
F#

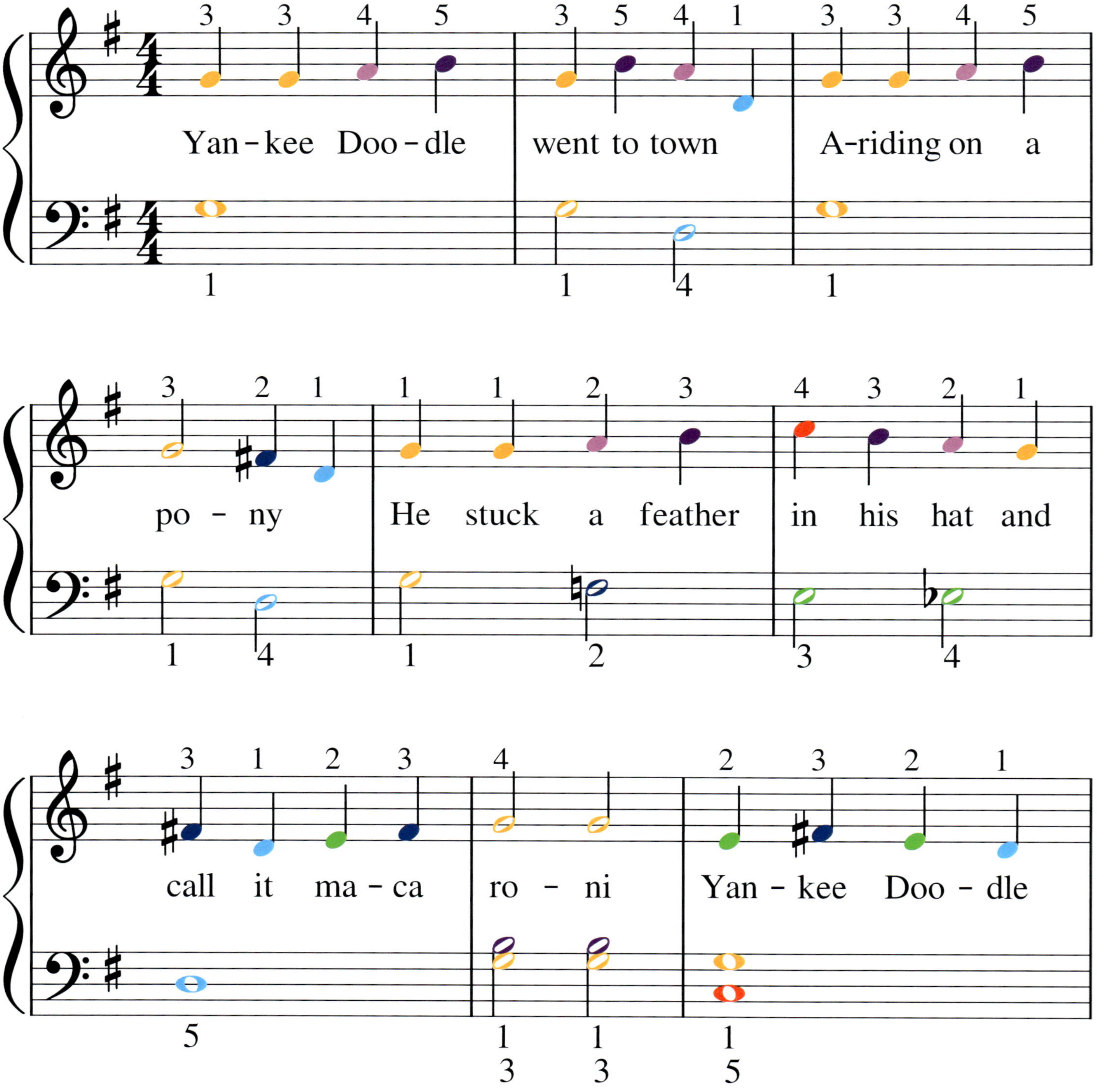
Yan-kee Doo-dle went to town A-riding on a
po - ny He stuck a feather in his hat and
call it ma-ca ro - ni Yan - kee Doo - dle

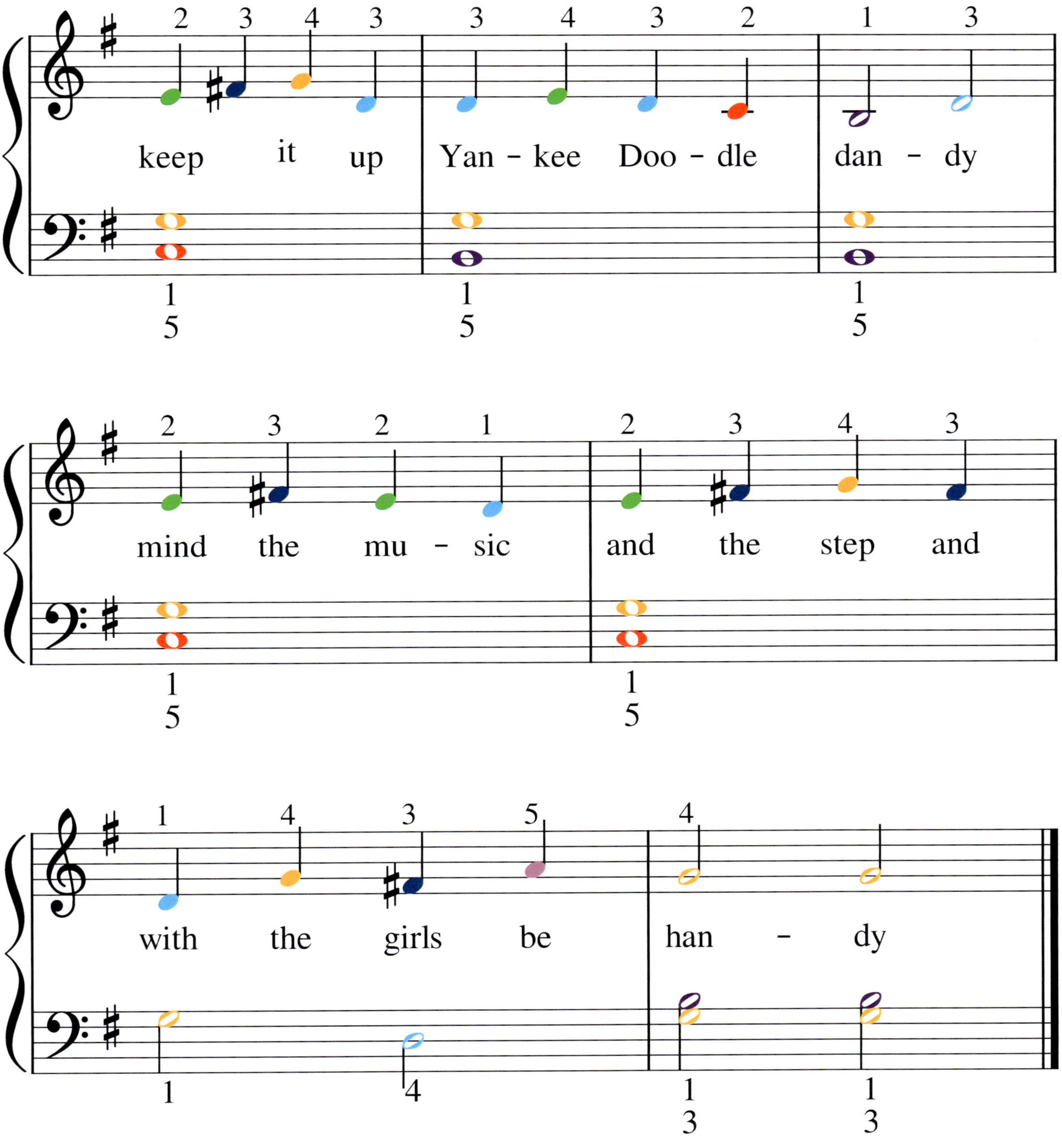
keep it up Yan - kee Doo - dle dan - dy
mind the mu - sic and the step and
with the girls be han - dy

Lullaby

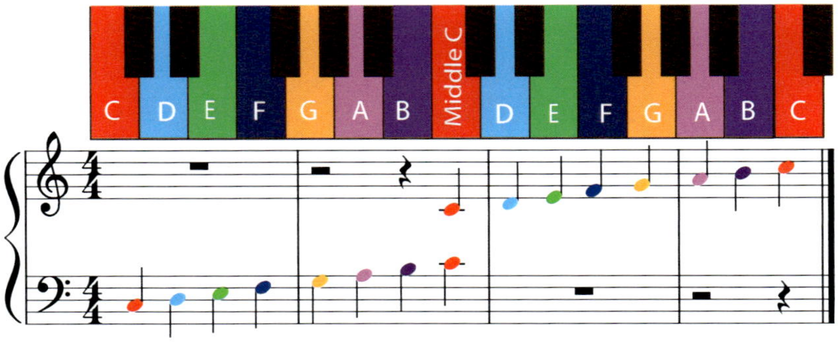
C D E F G A B Middle C D E F G A B C

1 3 1 3 1 3
E E G E E G E G
C G C G
5 1
5 4 3 3 2 1 2 3 2 1 2
C H A A G D E F D D E
C G D G D G
4 1
3 1 3 3 2 1 3 4 1
F D F H A G H C C C
D G D G F E C
4 1 4 1 2 3 5

5 5 3 4 3 1 3 4 5
A A F G E C F G A
C A C G D E F
5 1 5 1 4 3 2
4 1 5 5 3 4 3 1
C C A A F G E C
E3 C5 C A E C
5 1 3 5
4 3 2 1
F E D C
D G F E3 C5
4 1 2

Hush Little Baby

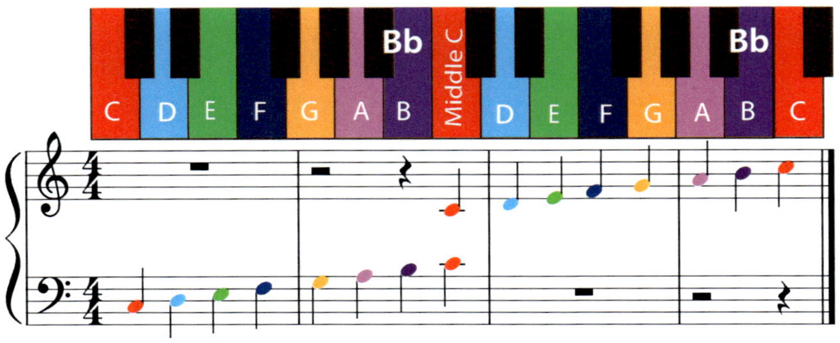
Bb
Middle C
Bb
C D E F G A B
D E F G A B C

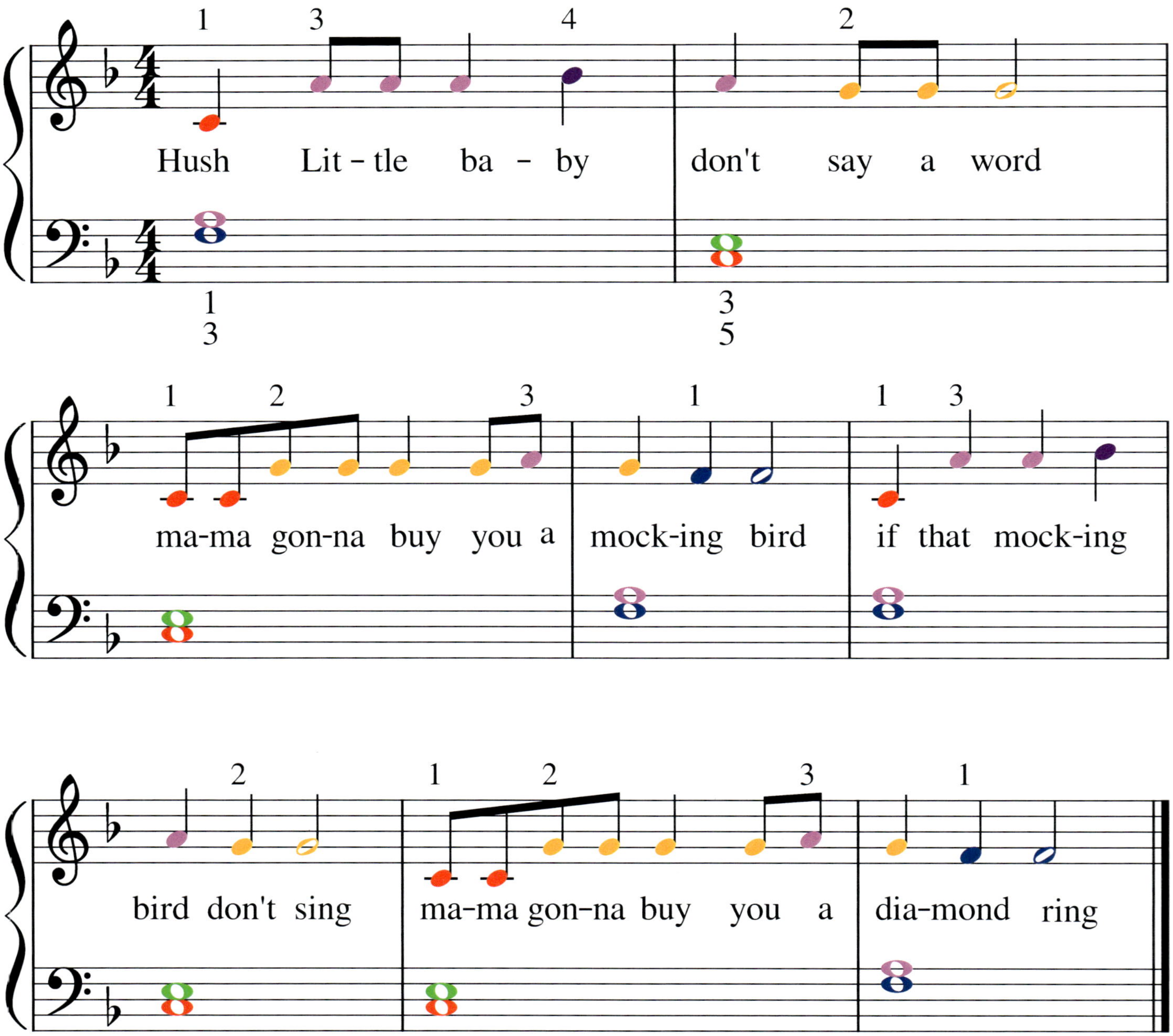
Hush Lit - tle ba - by don't say a word
ma-ma gon-na buy you a mock-ing bird if that mock-ing
bird don't sing ma-ma gon-na buy you a dia-mond ring

Skip to My Lou

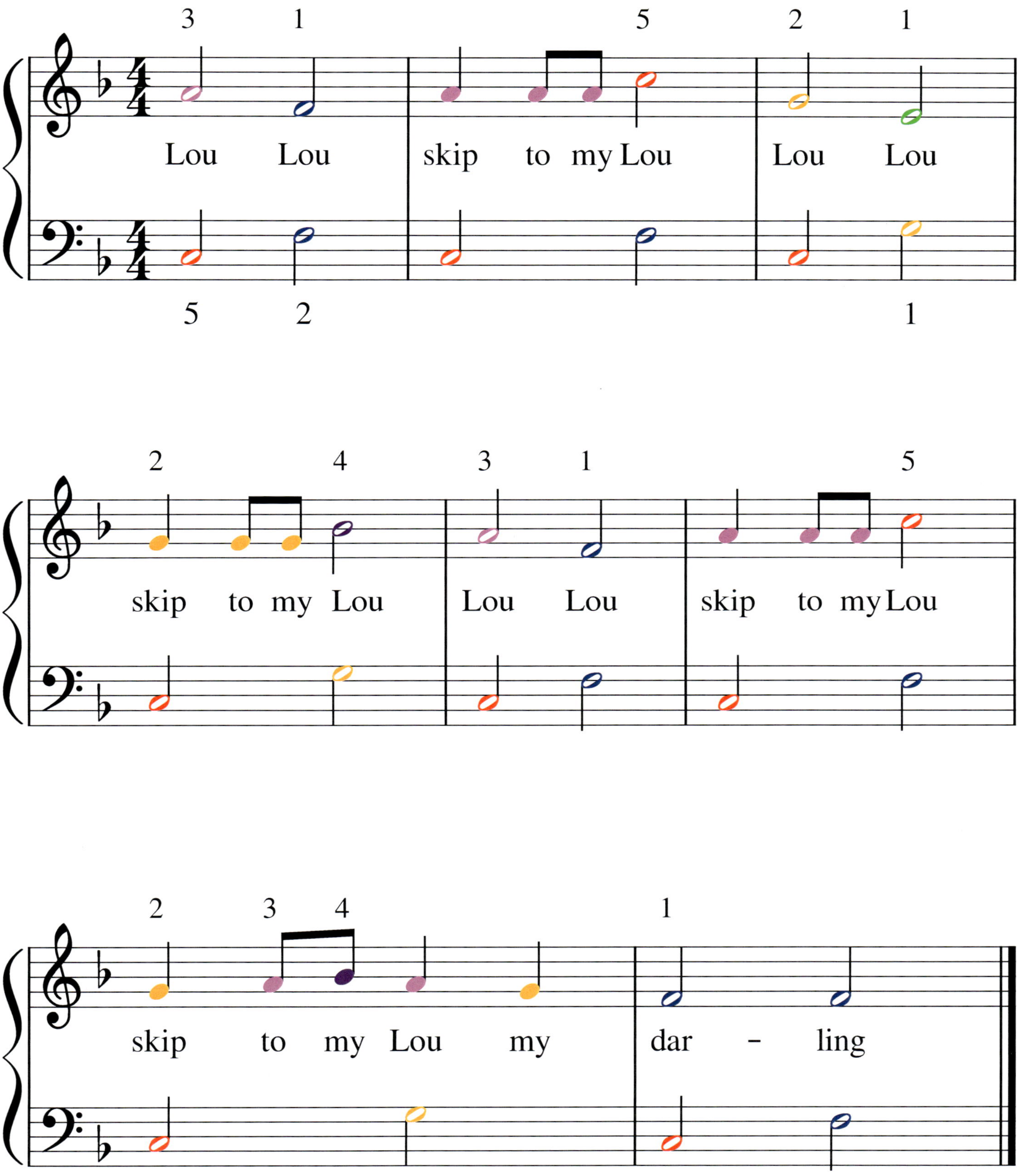
3 1 5 2 1
Lou Lou skip to my Lou Lou Lou
5 2 1
2 4 3 1 5
skip to my Lou Lou Lou skip to my Lou
2 3 4 1
skip to my Lou my dar - ling

Kum Ba Yah

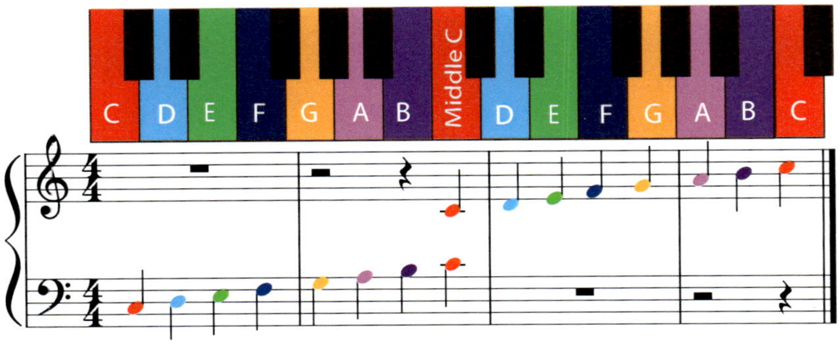
C D E F G A B Middle C D E F G A B C

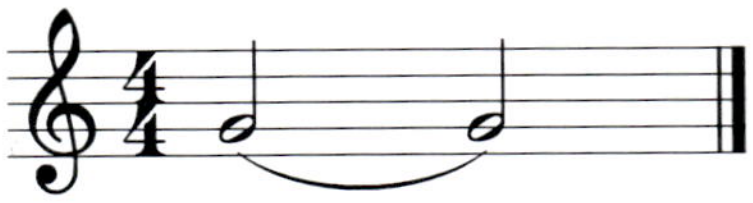

Tie: A tie is a curved lined musical notation that connects two of the same notes and only the first note is played.

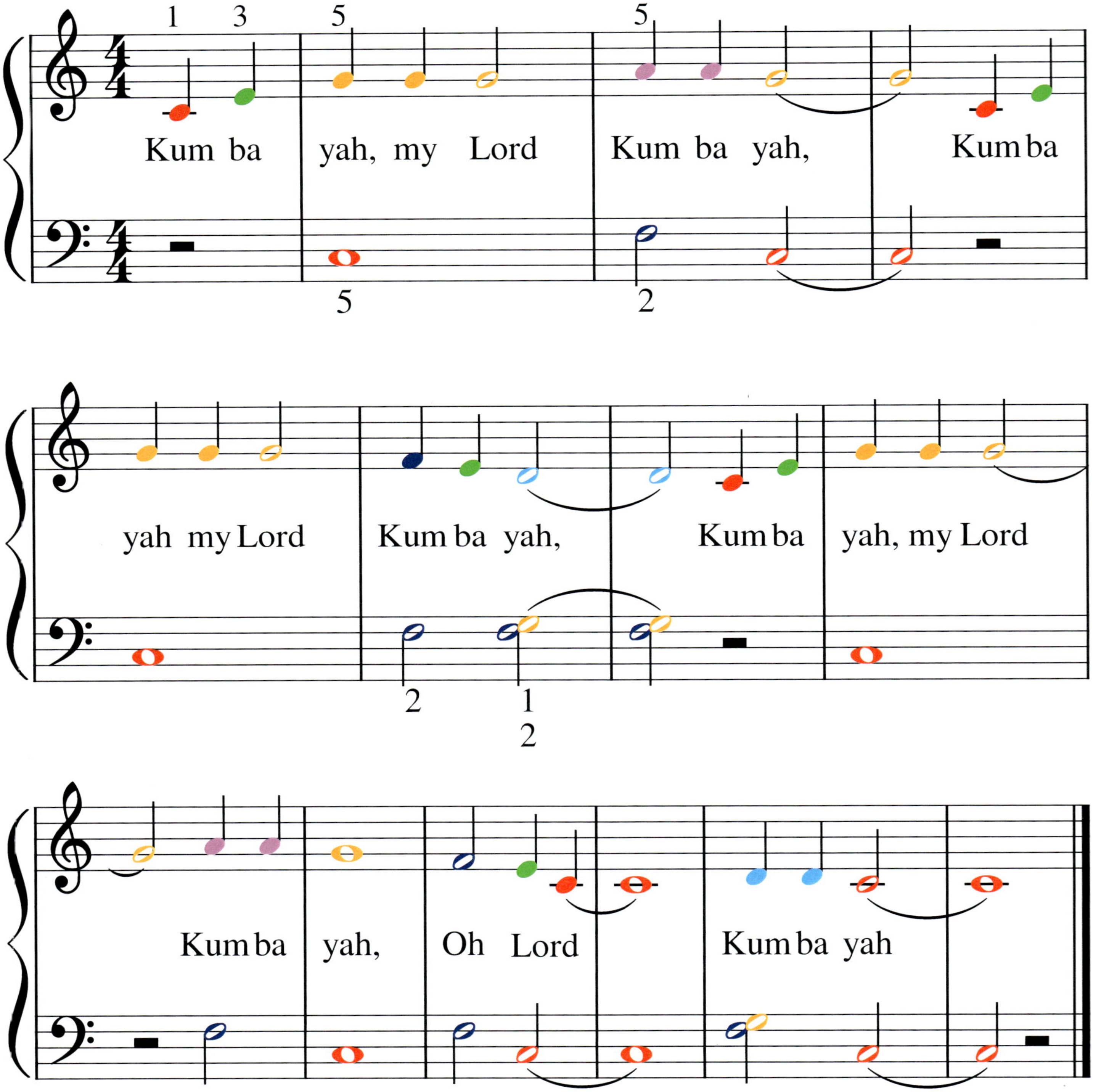
1 3 5 5
Kum ba yah, my Lord Kum ba yah, Kum ba
5 2
yah my Lord Kum ba yah, Kum ba yah, my Lord
2 1
2
Kum ba yah, Oh Lord Kum ba yah

The Muffin Man

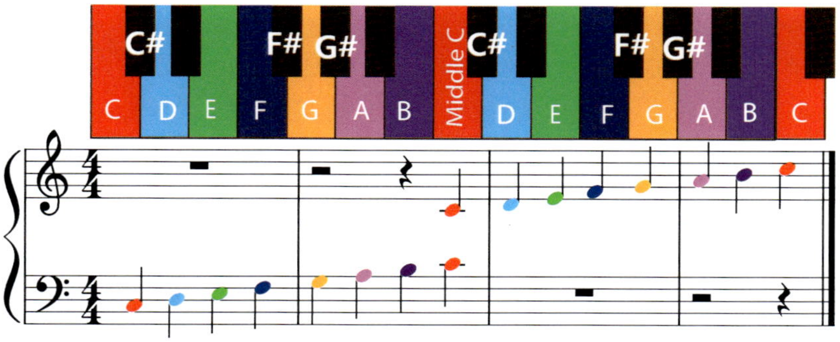
C#
F#
G#
C#
F#
G#
C
D
E
F
G
A
B
Middle C
D
E
F
G
A
B
C

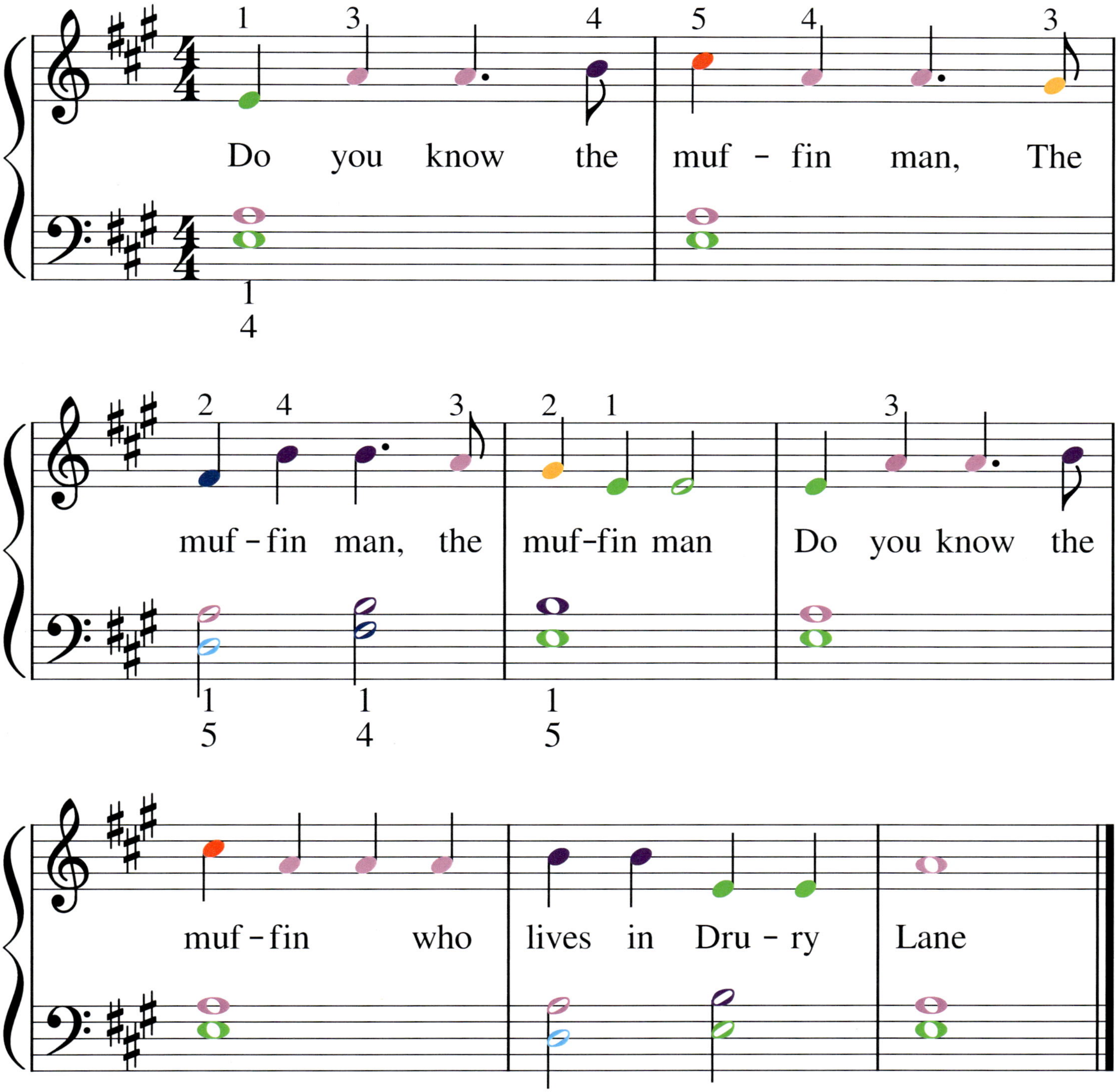
Do you know the muf - fin man, The
muf - fin man, the muf-fin man Do you know the
muf - fin who lives in Dru - ry Lane

We Wish You a Merry Christmas

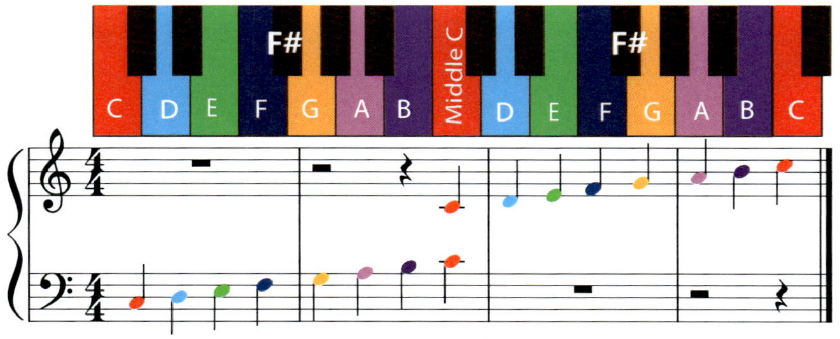
F#
F#
C D E F G A B
Middle C
D E F G A B C

We wish you a Mer-ry Christ-mas we
wish you a Mer-ry Christ-mas we wish you a Mer-ry
Christ-mas and a hap-py New Year! Good

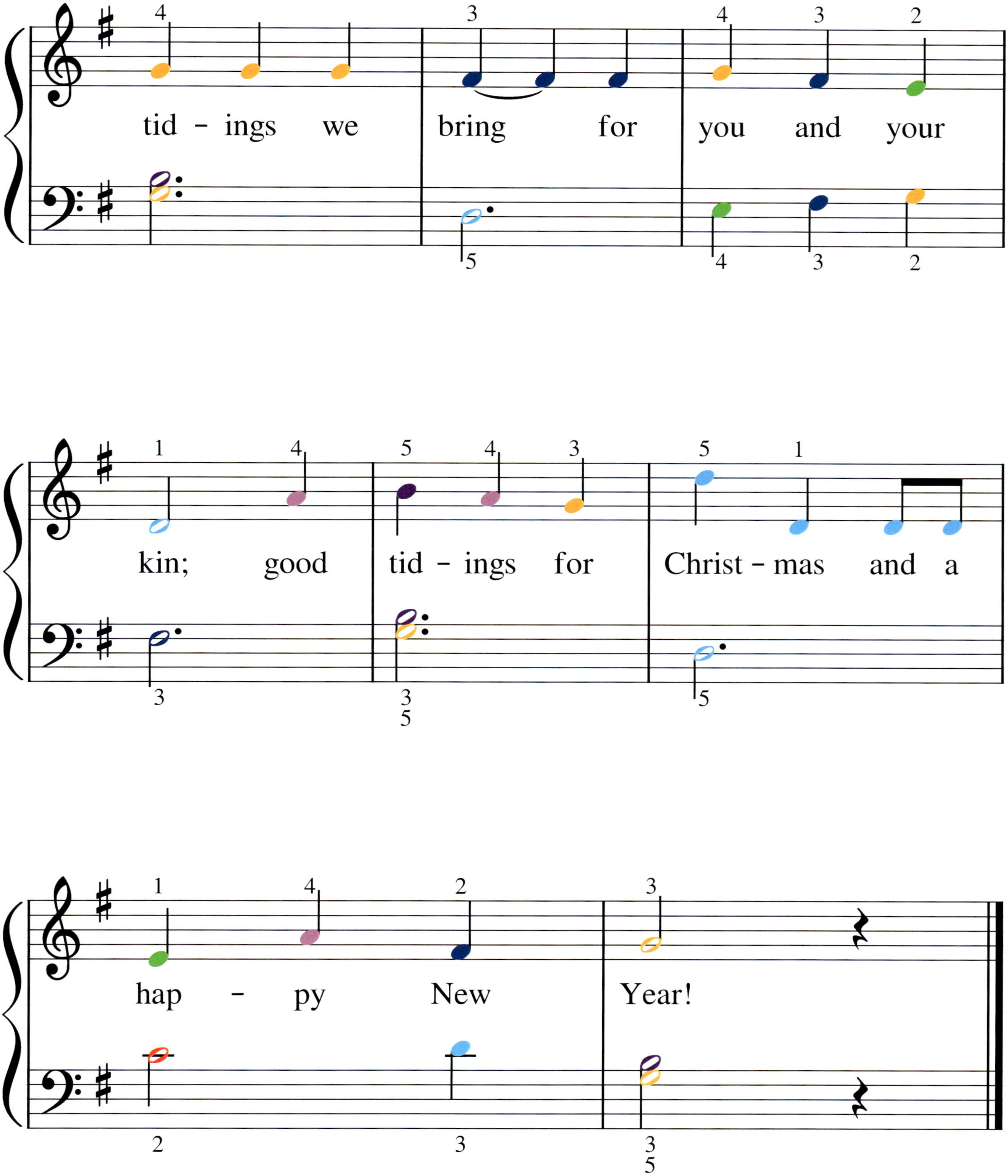
tid - ings we bring for you and your
kin; good tid - ings for Christ - mas and a
hap - py New Year!

Girls and Boys

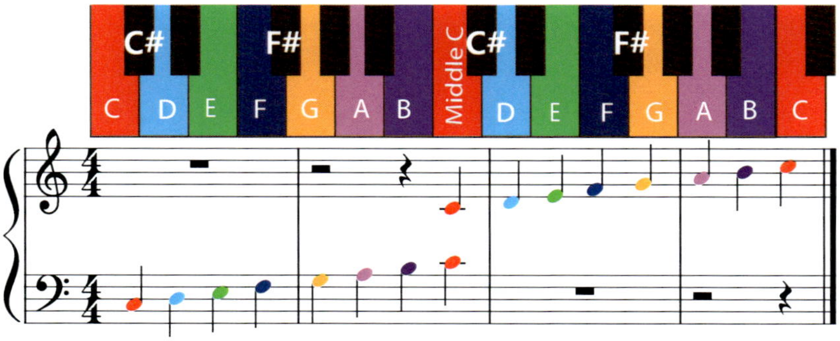
C#
F#
Middle C
C#
F#
C D E F G A B
D E F G A B C

5 3 4 2 1
Girls and boys come out to play The moon doth
3 1
5 4
4 5
shine as bright as day leave your sup-per and leave your
sleep come to your play fel-lows into the street

A Tisket A Tasket

A tisk - et A task - et A green and yell - ow bask - ket I
wrote a lett - er to my mommy on the way I dropped it. I
dropped it I dropped it and on the way I dropped it A
lit - tle gir - lie picked it up and put it in her pock - ket

Bingo

F#
F#
C
D
E
F
G
A
B
Middle C
D
E
F
G
A
B
C

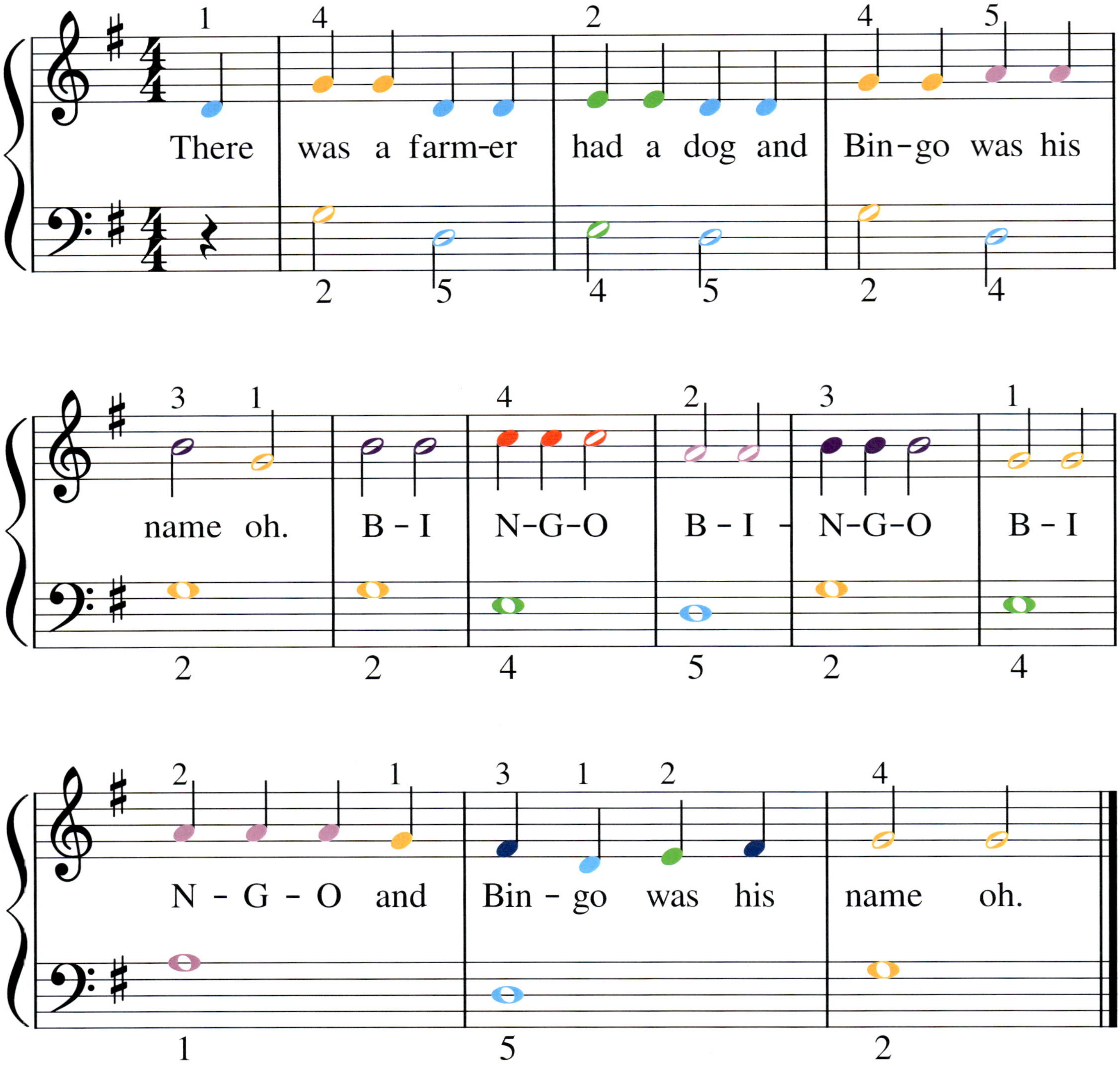
There was a farm-er had a dog and Bin-go was his
name oh. B - I N-G-O B - I - N-G-O B - I
N - G - O and Bin - go was his name oh.

Scarborough Fair

Tie: A tie is a curved lined musical notation that connects two of the same notes and only the first note is played.

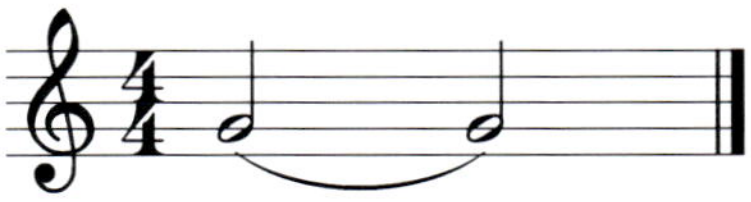

Are you going to Scar - bor-ough Fair? Pars - ley
sage rose - ma - ry and thyme re - mem - ber
me to one who lives there.... she once
was a true love of mine.....

Oranges and Lemons

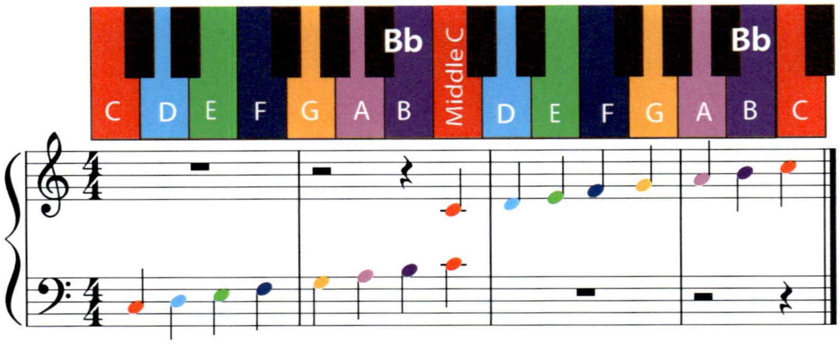
Bb
Middle C
Bb
C D E F G A B
D E F G A B C

5 3 1 2 3 4
oran - ges and le - mons says the bells of Saint
5 2
Cle - ments you owe me five far - things say the
bells of Saint Mar - tin's

Pop Goes the Weasel

F#
F#
C D E F G A B
Middle C
D E F G A B C

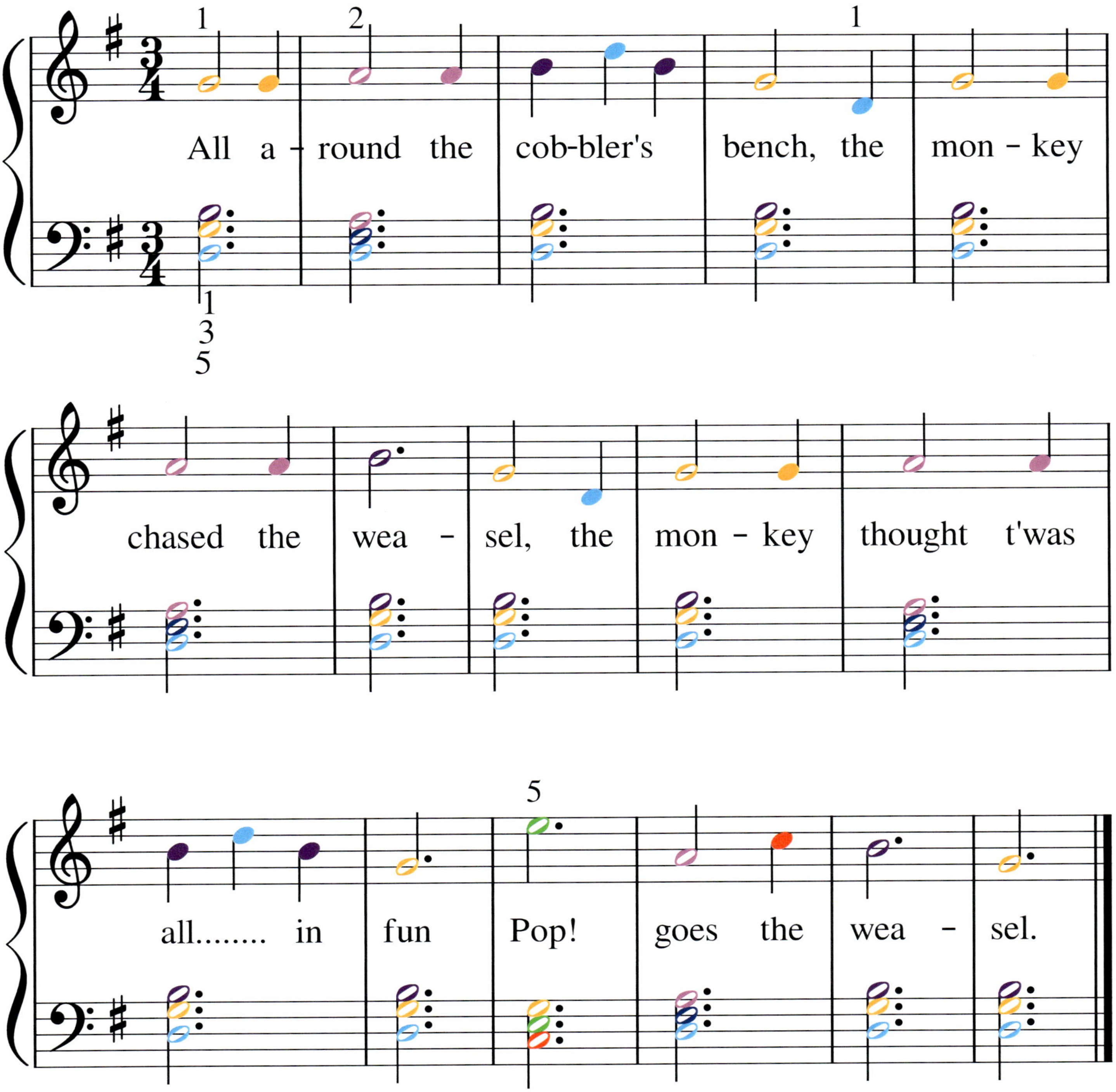
1 2 1
All a - round the cob-bler's bench, the mon - key
1
3
5
chased the wea - sel, the mon - key thought t'was
5
all........ in fun Pop! goes the wea - sel.

Coming Round the Mountain

C# F# G# C# F# G#
C D E F G A B Middle C D E F G A B C
She'll be
com - in 'round the
moun-tain when she
comes
She'll be
com - in 'round the
moun - tain she'll be
comes'
she'll be

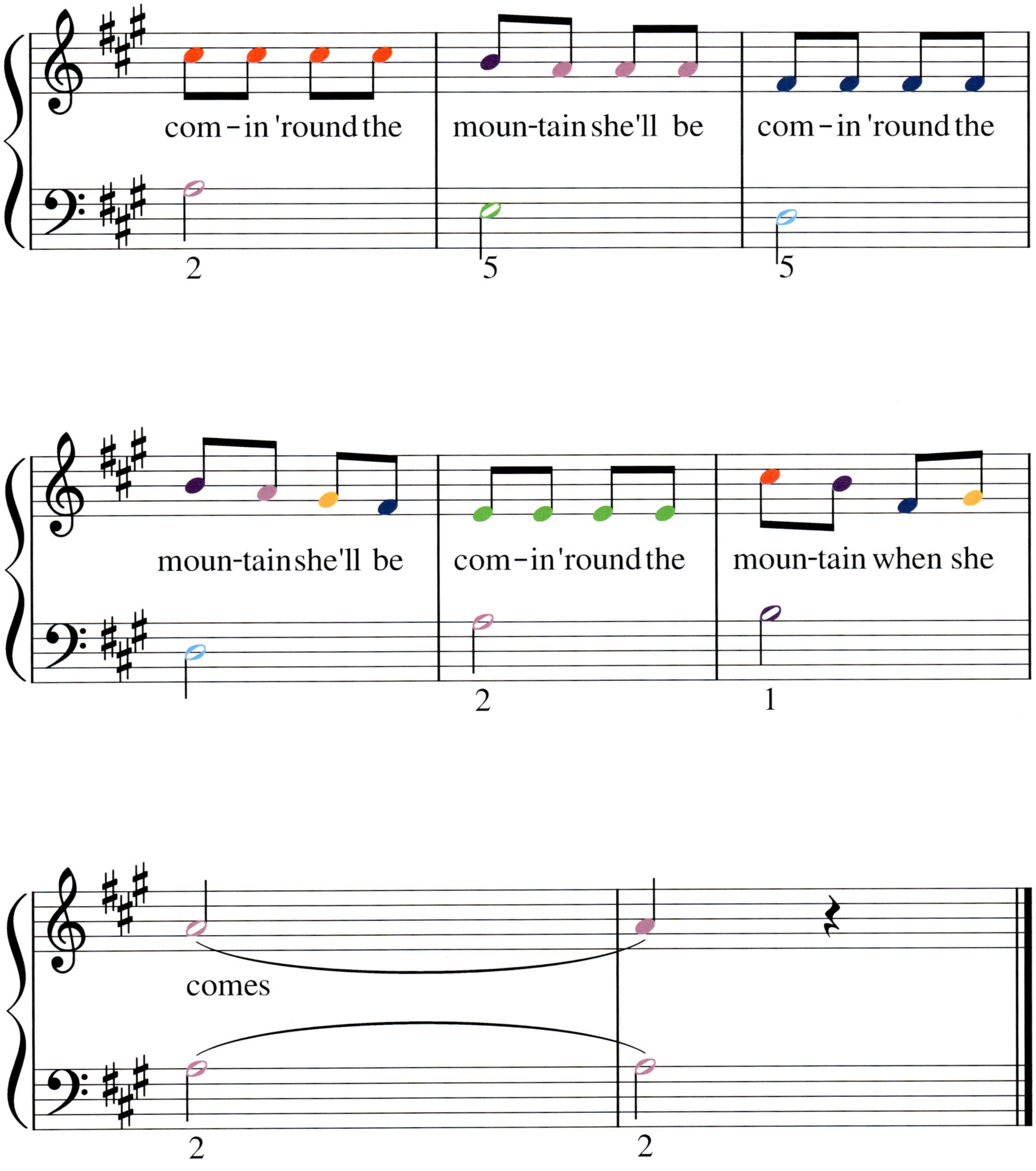
com - in 'round the
moun-tain she'll be
com - in 'round the
2
5
5
moun-tain she'll be
com - in 'round the
moun-tain when she
2
1
comes
2
2

Silent Night

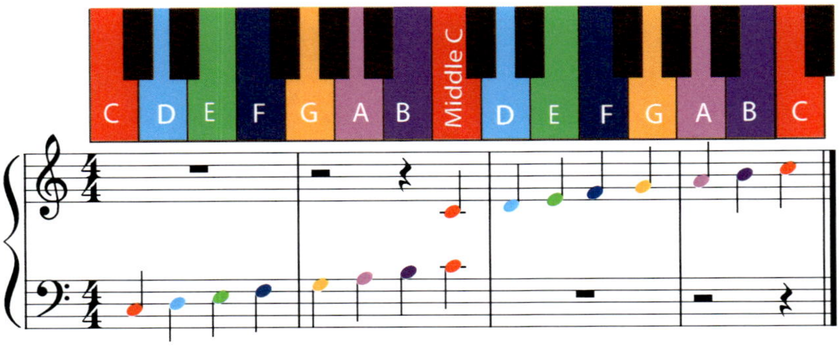
C D E F G A B Middle C D E F G A B C

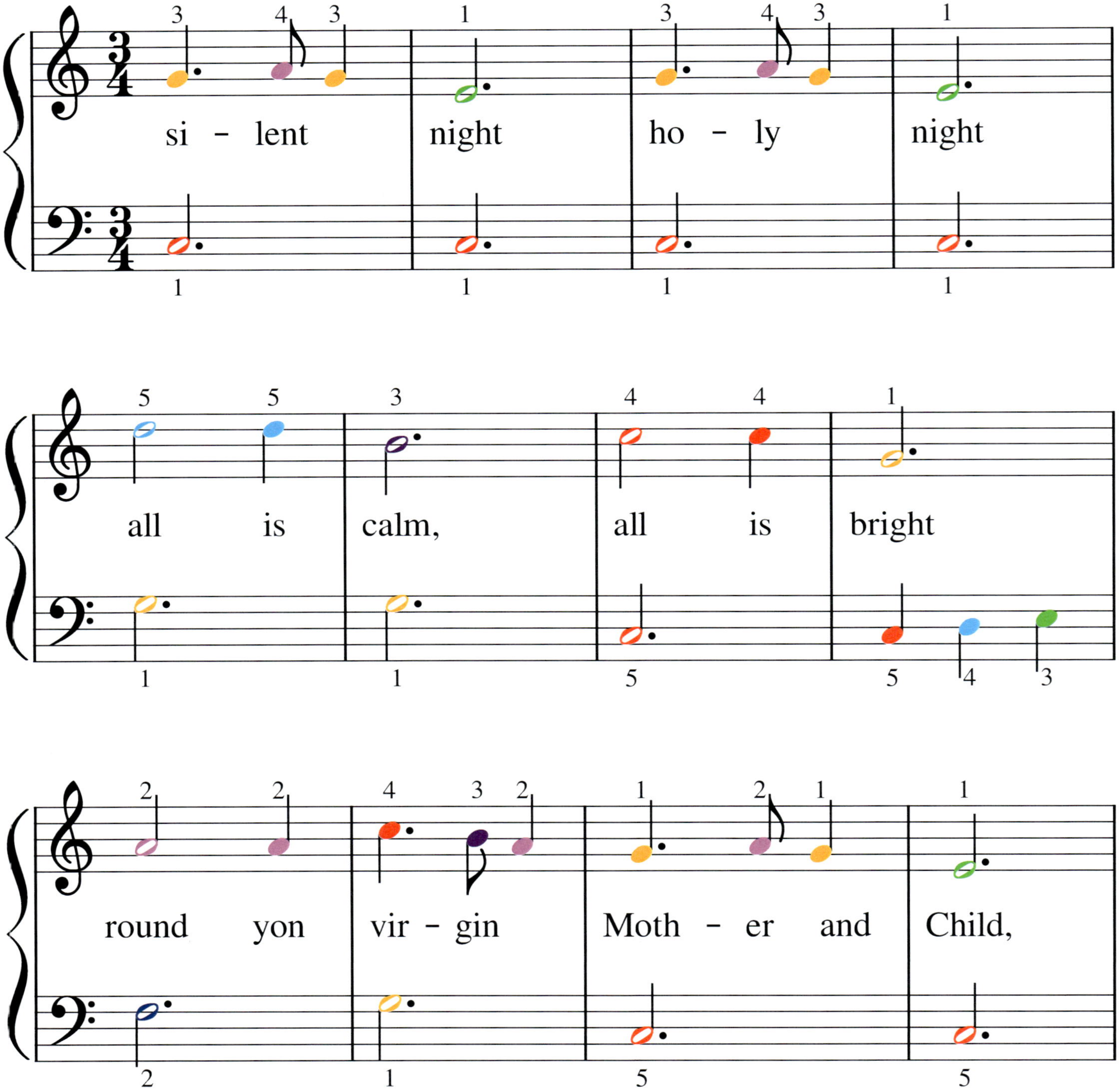
si - lent night ho - ly night
all is calm, all is bright
round yon vir - gin Moth - er and Child,

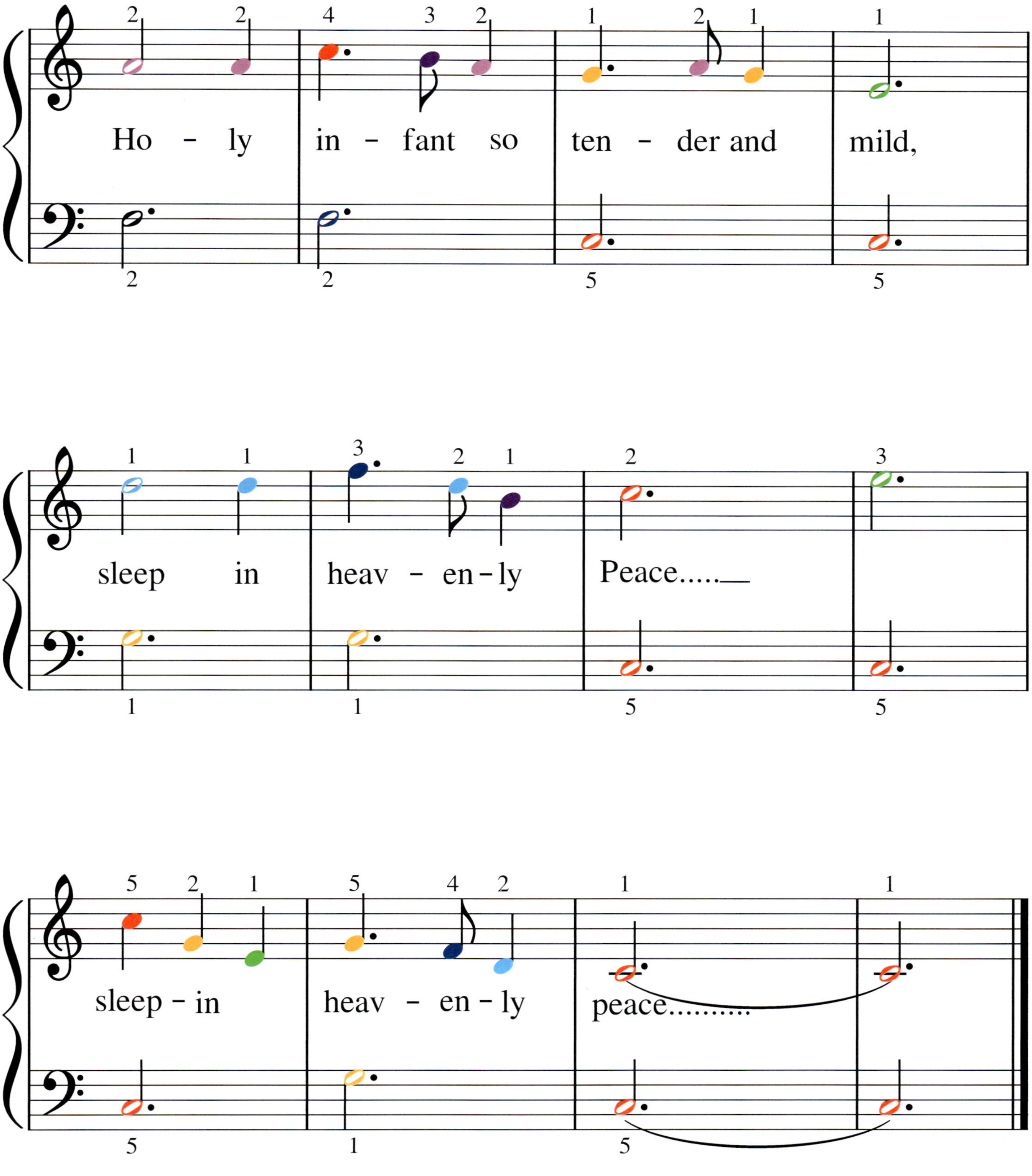
Ho - ly in - fant so ten - der and mild,
sleep in heav - en - ly Peace.....
sleep - in heav - en - ly peace..........

English Country Garden

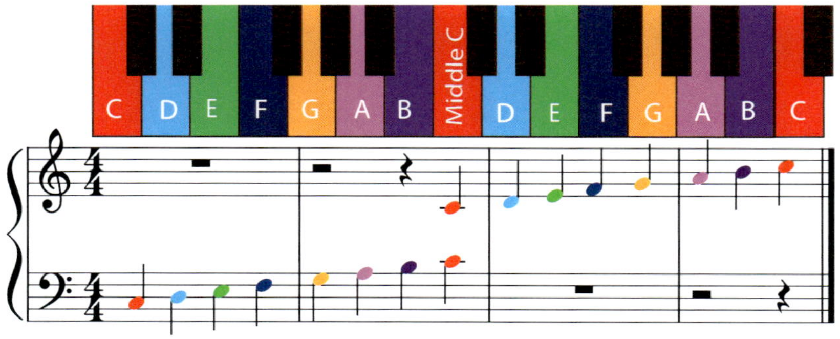
C D E F G A B
Middle C
D E F G A B C

How ma-ny kinds of
sweet flo-wers grow in an
En-glish coun-try
Gar-d-en
I'll tell you now of
some that I know and those I
miss you'll sure ly
Par-do-n

Daffodils heart's ease and flox
Mea-dow-sweet and lady smoc-ks
Gen-tain lu-pine
and tall holl-hocks Roses
fox gloves
snowdrops blue forget nots
In an English
Gar - d-en

Humpty Dumpty

Tips:
Humpty Dumpty song is in 6/8 time signature. Remember to count as 1, 2, 3, 4, 5, 6.

1 3 2 4 1 2 3 4 1 3 2 4
Hum - pty Dum-pty sat on a wall Hum - pty Dum - pty
5 2 1 5 5 2
5 3 1 2 1 3 2 4 1 2 3 4
had a great fall All the king's horses and all the king's men
5 2 1 2 1 5
3 1 4 3 3 2 1 2
couldn't put Humpty together again
5 2 1 5

Row Row Row Your Boat

Row Row Row your boat song is in 6/8 time signature. Remember to count as 1, 2, 3, 4, 5, 6. Don't forget the **Bb** note.

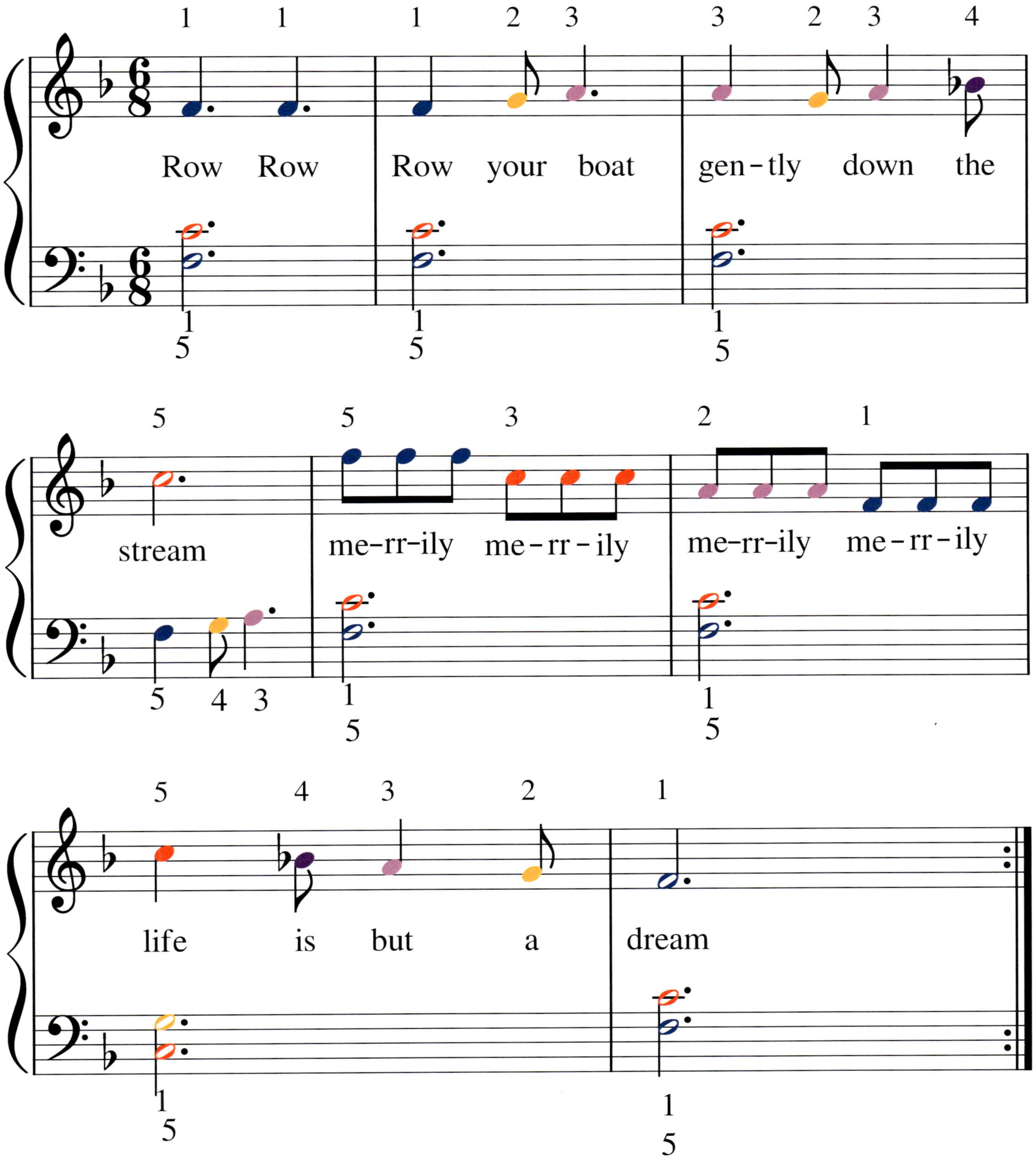
1 1 1 2 3 3 2 3 4
Row Row Row your boat gen-tly down the
1 5 1 5 1 5
5 5 3 2 1
stream me-rr-ily me-rr-ily me-rr-ily me-rr-ily
5 4 3 1 5 1 5
5 4 3 2 1
life is but a dream
1 5 1 5

If You're Happy

1 4 3 4 5 1
If you're hap - py and you know it clap your hands if you're
2 5
5 1 2 3
hap - py - and you know it clap your hands if you're
5 2
4 1 4 3 2 1 3
hap - py and you know it and you really want to show it if you're
1 2 4
4 3 2 1 2 3
hap - py and you know it clap your hands.
1 5 2

The Itsy Bitsy Spider

The itsy bitsy spi - der went up the water
spout down came the rain and washed the spider
out out came the sun and dried up all the rain Now the itsy bitsy
spi - der went up the spout again

The Farmer in the Dell

Tie: A tie is a curved lined musical notation that connects two of the same notes and only the first note is played.

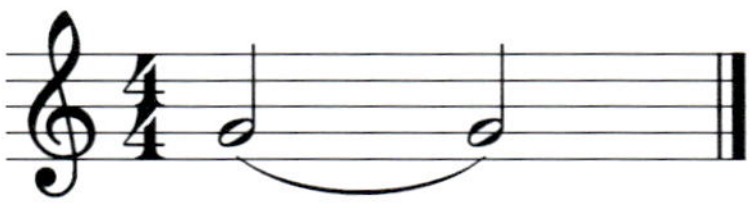

The farm - er in the dell, the farm - er
in the dell,
Heigh ho the der - ry
oh the farm - er in the dell

Head Shoulders Knees and Toes

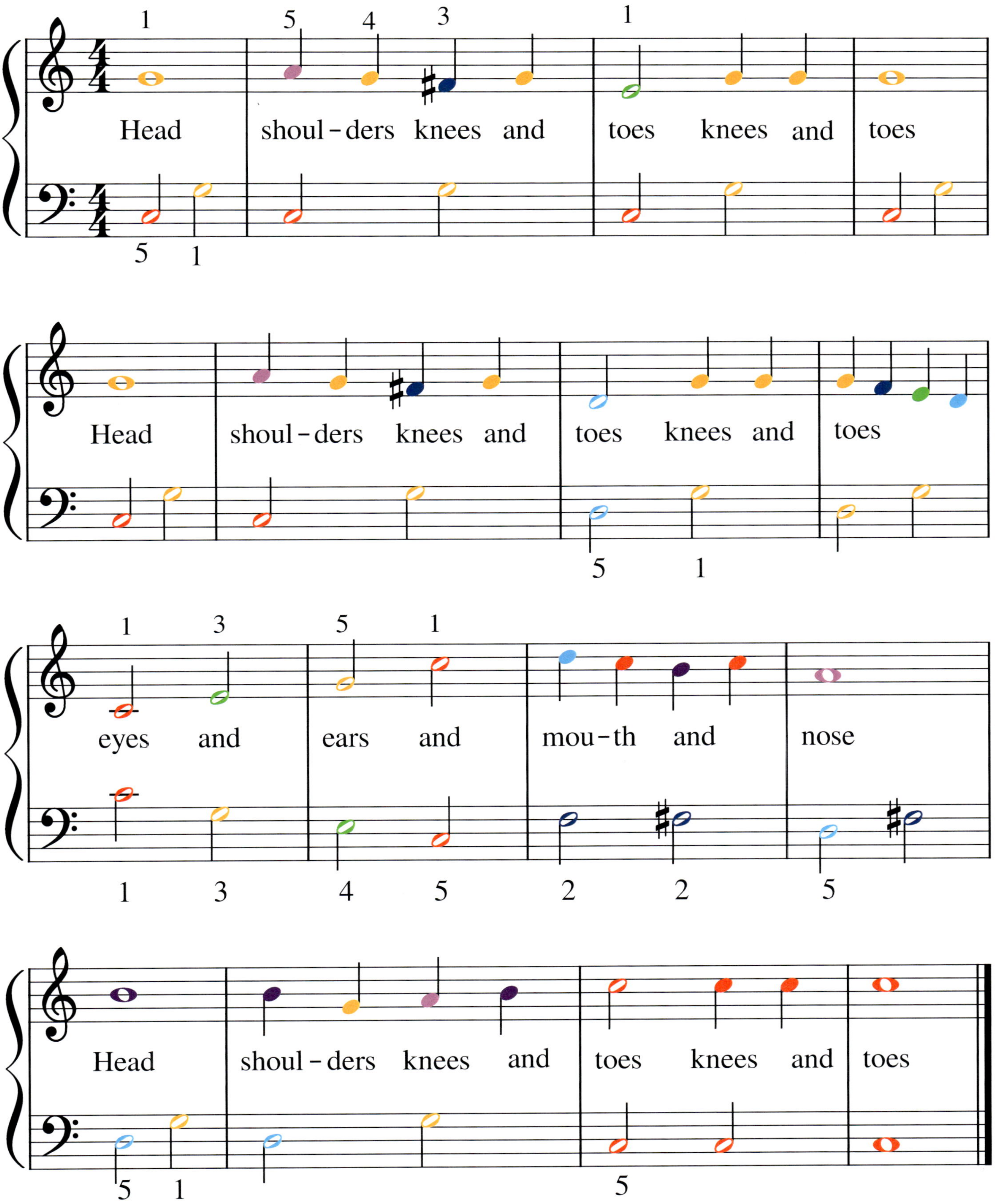
Head shoul-ders knees and toes knees and toes
Head shoul-ders knees and toes knees and toes
eyes and ears and mou-th and nose
Head shoul-ders knees and toes knees and toes

I Come from Alabama

1 2 3 4 5
Oh I come from Al - a ba - ma with my ban - jo on my
1
5
knee I'm goin to Loui - si - a - na My - true love for to
1
4
see Oh! Su - san-na oh don't you cry for me Oh! I
1
1 5 4 3 2
5 5
come from Al - a ba - ma with my ban - jo on my knee

Lavender's Blue

1 5 5
La - ven-der's blue dil-ly dil-ly La - ven-der's green
5 3 1 5 3 1
When I am king, dil-ly dil-ly you shall be queen.
Who told you so dil-ly dil-ly who told you so?
Twas my own heart dil-ly dil-ly that told me so.

Polly Put the Kettle On

Pol-ly put the kett-le on Pol-ly put the ket-tle on
Pol-ly put the ket-tle on We'll all have tea
Su-key take it off a-gain Su-key take it off a-gain
Su-key take it off a-gain They've all gone a-way

Molly Malone

In Dublin's fair city Where the girlsare so pre-tty I
first set my eyes on sweet Mo – lly Ma – lone As
she wheeled her wheelbarrow through streetsboard and
narrow crying cockles and mussels a – livealive oh!

Tom Dooly

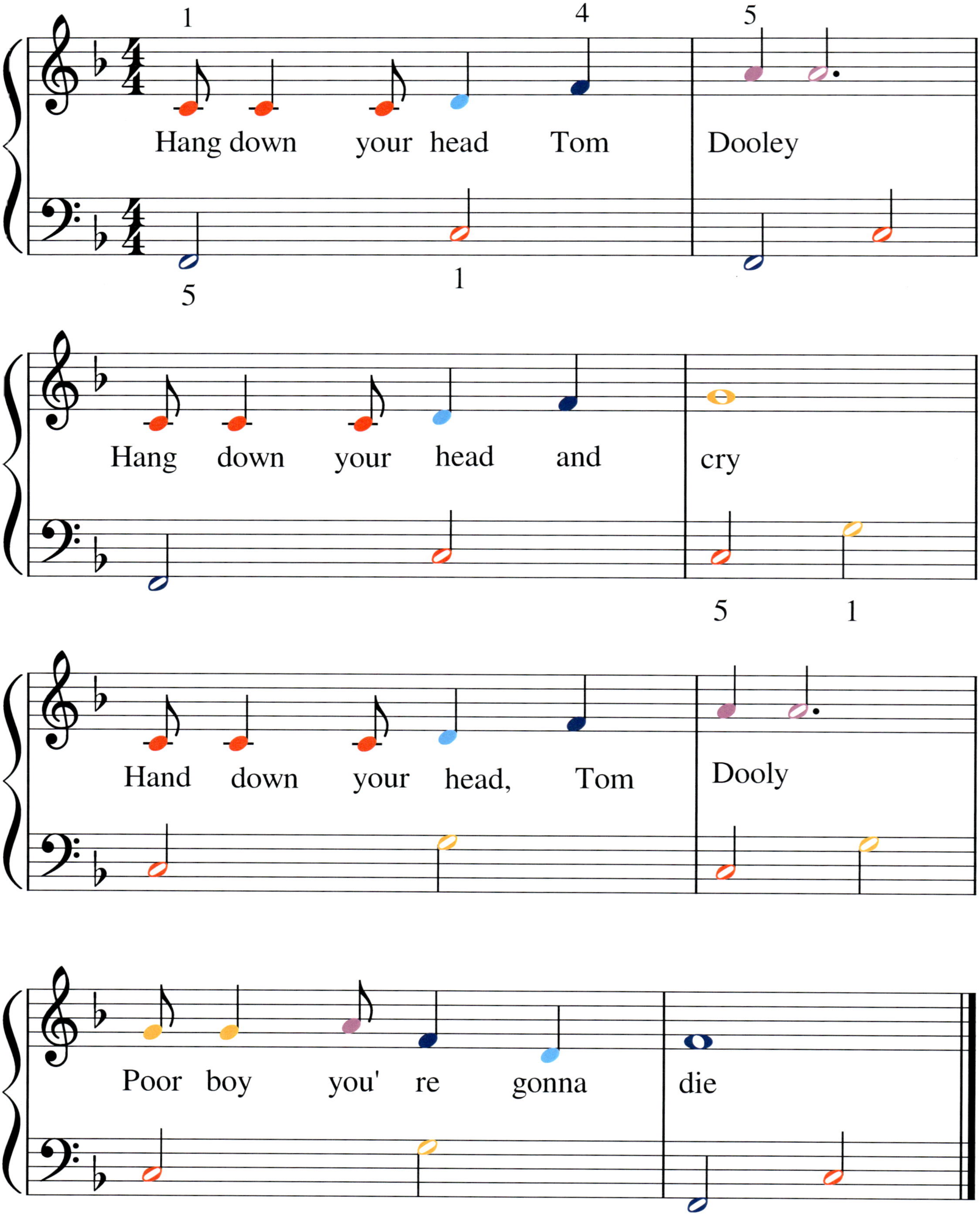
1 4 5
Hang down your head Tom Dooley
5 1
Hang down your head and cry
5 1
Hand down your head, Tom Dooly
Poor boy you' re gonna die

Red River Valley

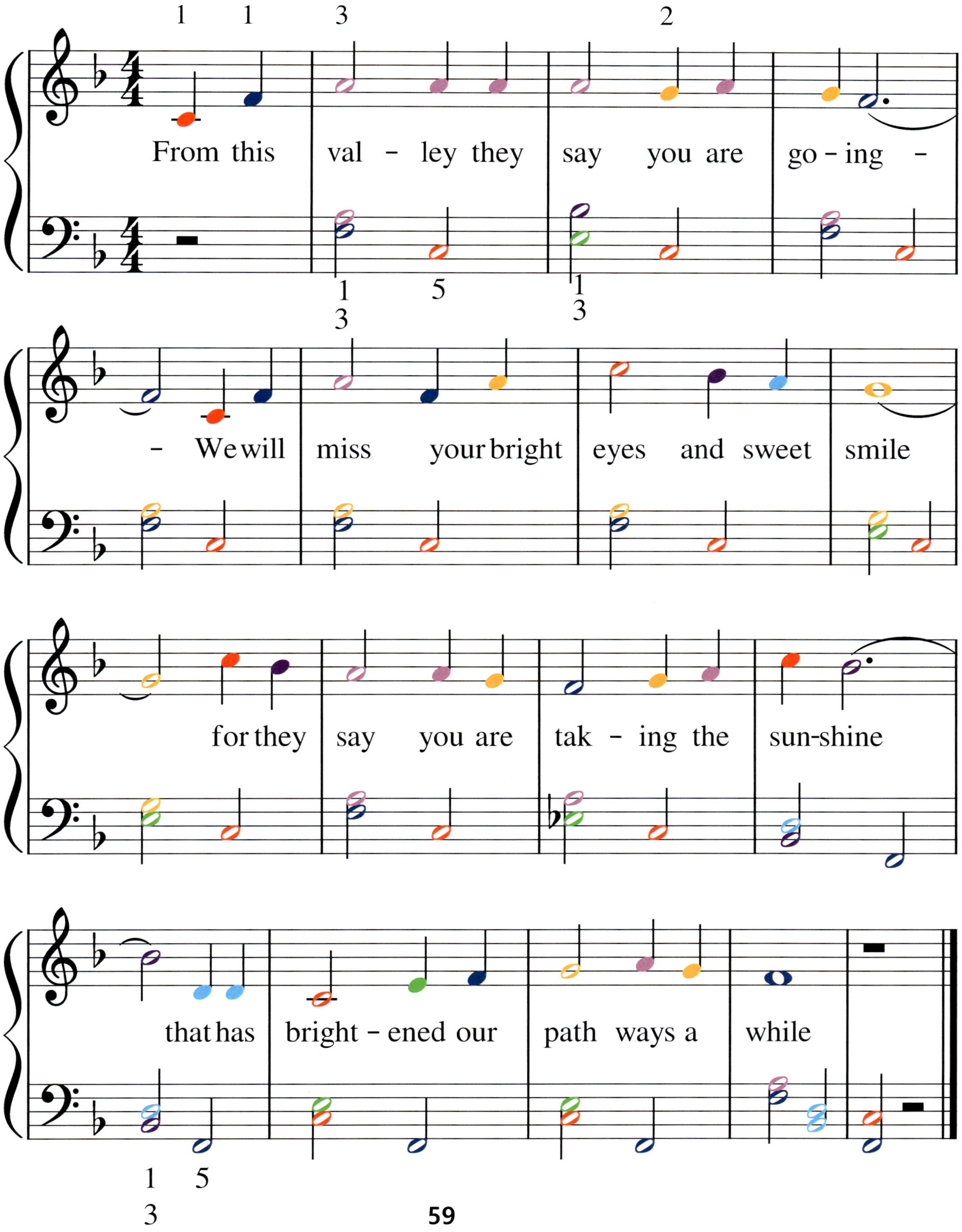
1 1 3 2
From this val - ley they say you are go - ing -
1 5 1
3 3
- We will miss your bright eyes and sweet smile
for they say you are tak - ing the sun-shine
that has bright - ened our path ways a while
1 5
3

Für Elise

Ludwig van Beethoven

mp

mp - Stands for Mezzo-Piano which means play "moderately soft".

Camptown Races

4 3 2
Camp-town la - dies sing this song Doo-da Doo-da
1 5 1 4
Camp-town race track's five miles long oh, do doo-da day
Goin'to run all night Goin'to run all day bet my money
1 5
on the bobtail-nag some - body bet on the gray

Hickory Dickory Dock

3 4 5
Hick-o-ry dick-o-ry dock The mouse ran up the
5
1
2
4 2
clock The clock struck one, the mouse ran down;
1 2 1
1 2 4 3 2 1
Hick - o - ry dick - o - ry dock

When the Saints Go Marching In

1 3 4
5
Oh, when the
saints
go march-ing
in
1 3 5
1 3 5
Oh, when the
saints go
march - ing
in
oh Lord, I
want to
be in
that number
when the
1 3 5
saints go
march - ing
in.